D1106356

Merry Christmas
Grandpa

Love,
Kurt

1970

#70,091

12⁵⁰

THE PUEBLO INCIDENT

Books by Admiral Daniel V. Gallery

THE PUEBLO INCIDENT
THE BRINK
STAND BY TO START ENGINES
8 BELLS AND ALL'S WELL
NOW HEAR THIS
TWENTY MILLION TONS UNDER THE SEA
CLEAR THE DECKS

THE
PUEBLO
INCIDENT

Rear Admiral Daniel V. Gallery, Ret.

DOUBLEDAY & COMPANY, INC.   GARDEN CITY, NEW YORK   1970

Library of Congress Catalog Card Number 71–97709
Copyright © 1955, 1970 by Daniel V. Gallery
All Rights Reserved
Printed in the United States of America
First Edition

CONTENTS

*To those who have lost their lives on ships
defending their country at sea*

If the world survives much longer in this atomic age, three dates in the past twenty-seven years will stand out for future students of U.S. history. They are December 7, 1941; September 2, 1945 and January 23, 1968.

F.D.R. called the first a day that will live in infamy. But on it, the sleeping giant in these United States woke up. We struggled up from the mud of Pearl Harbor to smash the unholy alliance of Hitler and the Japs, which seemed at that time destined to conquer the world.

The second date marks the high point in the history of the United States as a world power. It's when World War II ended with unconditional surrender on the quarter-deck of the U.S.S. *Missouri*. At that moment, the United States was by far the strongest and most respected country in this world.

The third one, less than thirty years later, is a shameful milestone in the decline and fall of the United States. On that date, the U.S.S. *Pueblo*, without firing a shot, was boarded, captured, and surrendered to a rabble of gooks off the coast of Korea.

The Navy had a major role in events on all of these three dates. This is natural because control of the seas has played a vital part in the growth of the country to greatness. From the days of the Revolution to the surrender on the *Missouri*, the Navy's part was a glorious one, reflecting what was happening in the country. The *Pueblo* reflects what is happening in it too.

The country and the Navy grew together from humble beginnings to the greatest in the world. Now that the country is becoming soft and decadent, the Navy is declining with it. The old virtues that made the United States great are being discarded. The country is drifting toward dangerous waters and dragging the Navy along with it.

The Navy is being swallowed up in the faceless bureaucracy of the Defense Department. Whiz kids and computers are taking over the job of running the ships at sea. In this day of hippies and draft card burners, patriotism is for squares, and "brass hat" has become a dirty word.

Young officers who were lads in high school when the Japs surrendered are now coming up for promotion to admiral. They are the products of the new system, born in the name of Unification and perfected by Mr. McNamara under the banner of "Cost Effectiveness." They are victims of a Frankenstein. They have been molded by it and have conformed—otherwise they wouldn't be coming up for promotion.

As one who spent his life in the old Navy and became a rear admiral in it, I think I'm entitled to speak my piece about what's happening to it now.

What follows in this book is the opinion of one who served in the Navy from 1917 to 1960. If it is out of tune with the times, perhaps it may at least be of historical interest to show how things used to be.

Throughout this book I use the word "gooks" in referring to the North Koreans. Some people object to this word.

By "gook" I mean precisely an uncivilized Asiatic Communist. I see no reason for anyone who doesn't fit this definition to object to the way I use it.

Rear Admiral Daniel V. Gallery, Ret.

THE PUEBLO INCIDENT

Since long before the days of sail, a ship of war has been regarded by civilized nations as a part of the country to which she belonged. Size and class had nothing to do with this status. It applied equally to the nuclear carrier *Enterprise* or to a plodding oil tanker. Until the *Pueblo* affair, any man-o'-war flying our national colors and a Navy commission pennant was just as much a part of U.S. territory as the White House lawn.

It is ironic that of the hundreds of Navy ships of all sizes and shapes, the one that has won herself the most conspicuous place in the history of recent years was one of the smallest and least glamorous. Her very existence was more or less hush hush—until she hit the fan with a splurge that dwarfs anything ever done by the battleship *New Jersey*.

The *Pueblo* was a puny spit kit of 935 tons, 176 feet long. She had diesel engines that could drive her at 13 knots and mounted two 50-caliber machine guns, one forward and one aft. Her complement was 6 officers and 77 enlisted men.

She was a sort of an illegitimate stepchild at best. She

started out in 1944 as an Army craft. She cost 800,000 dollars and was designed to haul miscellaneous cargo to out-of-the-way places in the Pacific. Later she saw service in the South Korean Merchant Marine. In 1967 she was taken over by the Navy and fitted out to be an ELINT ship (ELINT=Electronics Intelligence). This conversion was budgeted to cost 5.3 million dollars but was later cut to 4.3 million.

The mission of such a ship is to snoop as close as the law allows to an "adversary's" coast and gather data on radar and radio transmissions. In this day and age, such data is of vital importance. The radio traffic that they tape is pay dirt for the black chamber experts of NSA (National Security Agency) who break codes. The dope she gets on radar frequencies, pulse repetition rates, IFF (Information, Friend or Foe) signals, and the location of radarsites can mean life or death to our fliers. What we find out from these electronic transmissions enables us to baffle enemy antiaircraft rockets and to get out missiles past their jammers. In the never-ending battle of wits to find countermeasures against enemy electronics, and counter-countermeasures to baffle the countermeasures he devises against ours, this stuff is grist for the mills of the black box designers. It was this sort of information gathered by ELINT ships off the coast of Cuba that tipped us off that the Russians were installing missiles in Cuba. Photo flights confirmed the suspicions of the electronic snoopers and led to the confrontation with Russia before they were ready for it. Had it not been for the snoopers, we might not have known of those missiles until after they were all installed, cocked, and ready to shoot. This information is so important that we maintain a squadron of a dozen or more such ships, although you never hear of them until they get in trouble—as the *Liberty* did, as well as the *Pueblo*.

These are commissioned Navy ships manned by regular

Navy crews, their credentials as a man-o'-war are just as good as the *Enterprise*. Theoretically they are under Navy operational control, but actually, it's hard to tell who they are working for—CIA, NSA, or DIA (Defense Intelligence Agency). When the *Liberty's* SOS was handed to the Sixth Fleet Operations officer during the Arab-Israeli war, his first question was, "What the hell is the Liberty?" Rear Admiral Epes in the *Enterprise* had exactly the same reaction when he got *Pueblo's* SOS. This highlights the divided responsibility for these ships, which, when the showdown comes, can result in no responsibility that can be pinned down.

The Russians are very much in this business too. Their fishing fleets off our Atlantic and Pacific coasts always have a couple of ELINT ships. It's easy to spot them because their topsides are loaded with radar dishes, antennas, and other Buck Rogers gear. Since the Russians are in cahoots with the North Koreans and Viet Cong, and supply them with most of their radars and missiles, one of the best places for us to get firsthand info on Russian electronics is off the Korean and Vietnam coasts.

This electronic snooping is a highly specialized business involving the black chamber boys of NSA, the CIA, and DIA. All had a finger in the *Pueblo's* pie, and all are outside regular Navy command channels. NSA and DIA report directly to Sec Def. The CIA is under nobody—except maybe the President. This resulted in divided responsibility all down the line, clear to the bridge of the little ship itself.

Spying is an ancient and dishonorable trade practiced by all civilized nations since the dawn of history. It involves acquiring military information of all kinds; plans of operations; order of battle; technical data on weapons; and breaking codes. Anything goes in it, including stealing, lying, bribery and, er . . . "liquidating" opponents.

Legally, a spy is a person who penetrates enemy lines in wartime seeking information in disguise. The penalty for getting caught is death, often by hanging. As a matter of protocol, spies who are in the military services of the enemy are usually shot—like Nathan Hale. Sometimes this courtesy is extended to civilian spies too—like Mata Hari.

Strictly speaking, spying occurs only in wartime. In peacetime, people engaged in espionage are known as secret agents, although in the paperback books and popular press, the term "spy" is loosely applied to them too. In recent years, rings of Communist secret agents reaching to very high places have been uncovered in the United States, Canada, and England. They stole some of our most closely guarded and vital atomic secrets. Many of the big ones got away and are now in Russia. We caught and electrocuted two of the small fry, the Rosenbergs, thus infuriating all the fellow travelers in this country.

A very important phase of espionage is code breaking, which goes on all the time, in peace and war. Breaking codes is a complex, almost magic art, practiced by highly specialized experts known as the black chamber. Intercepted code messages from all over the world are fed into the black chamber where they are analyzed, run through computers and mechanical brains, studied by screwball geniuses, and usually broken.

This can be the source of information vital to our national security. While we were still neutral in World War I, the British black chamber decoded the Zimmermann telegram. In this telegram Germany instructed her ambassador in Mexico to propose to the Mexicans that they declare war on the United States. Germany would join them; and at the end of the war, Mexico would be given Texas, New Mexico, and Arizona. This product of the black chamber had a great deal to do with persuading a reluctant President Wilson to declare war.

After the war, we had a very efficient black chamber in this country until Secretary of State Stimson found out about it in 1929. He broke it up on the grounds that "gentlemen do not read each other's mail." Incredible as it seems, the Secretary of State believed that international negotiations were conducted on a gentlemanly basis!

However, our black chamber got back in business again in time to break the Japanese codes and give us timely warning of Pearl Harbor. We didn't believe them—to our cost. But later, their work enabled us to win the Battle of Midway— the big turning point in the Pacific war—and still later, to intercept and shoot down the Commander in Chief of the Japanese Navy.

The OSS (Office of Strategic Services) handled our spy business during the war. Since then, the CIA has taken over. It reports directly to the President. Each of the military services has its own intelligence agency for gathering info of special interest to them. The Secretary of Defense also has his own agency, the DIA. The National Security Agency (NSA) runs the black chamber and reports directly to the Secretary of Defense. How all these cloak-and-dagger outfits fit together is quite a jigsaw puzzle and is, naturally, top secret. This makes it difficult for enemy agents to keep track of what they are all doing, and also makes it possible for all our people to blame everybody else when somebody goofs.

The *Pueblo* was trapped in this maze of divided responsibility. Much of the data that the *Pueblo* was picking up was of little immediate interest to the fleet. It had to go back to the various agencies in Washington for analysis and processing before it was of any use. Perhaps for this reason, *Pueblo* was not assigned to the Seventh Fleet, as all other

Navy ships in that area are. She was assigned to Commander Naval Forces, Japan. At the Navy court of inquiry it developed that, for all practical purposes, Naval Forces, Japan consisted of Rear Admiral Johnson, his staff on Yokosuka, and the U.S.S. *Pueblo*. The people for whom her electronics experts were working were in Washington. Whether they were Sec Def's whiz kids, the Navy, CIA, or NSA is open to argument.

Because of the special and secret character of her work, the ship itself was not organized the way any ordinary ship is. On all other Navy ships, the captain is the unquestioned boss of all hands on board. He can enter any space on the ship, and if he doesn't like what he sees, he can order it changed. This applies even to the atomic warhead magazines, on ships that have them, where you have to have a Q-clearance and practically be sprinkled with holy water before you can get in.

But on ELINT ships it was different. The captain was not the boss man in the holy of holies where the black boxes were installed. A young lieutenant, Harris, reporting directly to the ivory tower in Washington, was the boss there. The captain was admitted to those sacred precincts more or less by courtesy. But he wasn't cleared for knowledge of what went on in there, and he issued no orders there.

This violates Rule #1 of how a ship should be run. When the moment of truth comes, the captain holds the bag for the whole ship and everything in it. He *must* have positive control over everything and everyone on board. On the *Pueblo*, he didn't.

There is really no need for the captain to know all the details of what goes on in the holy of holies. Rule #1 of the security clearance business, especially for black chamber stuff, is "clearance is on a need-to-know basis only." The idea is that you can't inadvertently spill a secret if you don't know it. But aboard ship the captain should be entitled to know anything that *he* thinks he should know.

There were certain things about the secret equipment and papers that her captain, Commander Bucher, *did* need to know, whether cleared for it or not. He should have known how much of it there was, what means there were to destroy it, and how long this would take. It came out at the inquiry he was amazed at the amount of stuff they had. When it became evident they were going to be boarded and he went down to the holy of holies, he found the deck strewn with mattress covers jammed with secret papers.

Bucher understood very well the importance of being able to destroy his secret gear in the improbable event of capture. While he was fitting out the ship in Bremerton, he had officially requested scuttling and destruct devices. This request worked its way up to Washington through various bureaucratic channels and was pigeonholed. The reasons given now are lack of funds and nonexistence of satisfactory devices. Later Bucher tried, in Japan, to get TNT charges, which he could use as a last resort, but was talked out of it.

A major fact that accounts for the whole sorry business of the *Pueblo* is that nobody—but nobody—really believed it could happen. Piracy of a U. S. Navy ship on the high seas in A.D. 1968 was simply inconceivable.

Of course, after it happened, it seems inconceivable that we were all so naïve. But up to the moment when the *Pueblo's* flash came on the air, "They are firing at us"—everybody was.

One of the hard, cold facts of life at sea is that the captain is responsible for his ship, everything in it, and everything that happens to it. Certainly, no one from the ivory tower in Washington is going to step forward now and take the

blame for the loss of all that secret stuff on the *Pueblo*. As
long as nothing much was happening, this divided responsibility didn't matter much. But as soon as disaster strikes, responsibility for the whole show suddenly reverts back to the
captain. This is where it should have been unmistakably fixed
all the time.

This fuzzy division of responsibility extended clear up the
chain of command. Normally, any ship operating off the
Korean coast would work under Commander Seventh Fleet.
But not the *Pueblo!* She reported to the so-called Commander
Naval Forces, Japan. She was certainly in the bailiwick of
Commander Pacific Fleet, who works under Commander in
Chief, Pacific. But on account of the black chamber aspects
of her job, she was also working for ivory tower experts
back in Washington, who have no real responsibility for ships
at sea. The fleet commanders are responsible for the safety
of their ships and for helping them if they get in trouble.
If *Pueblo* had been a destroyer, there would have been no
question about shooting back or about giving her whatever
help she needed instantly. When the U.S.S. *Maddox* and
C. Turner Joy were attacked by Vietnam PT boats in the
Gulf of Tonkin in '64, our reaction was immediate and violent.
The fleet commanders were responsible for these ships and
had authority to act.

It turns out now that the fleet commander's control over
the *Pueblo* was nominal. When she got in trouble CINCPAC
(Commander in Chief of the Pacific Fleet) had to go to
Washington to get authority to act. The only agency in the
Defense Department that really had undivided responsibility
for the *Pueblo* was the Secretary of Defense Office, which
has over-all responsibility for everything. And fuzzy lines of
command to NSA and CIA might move it up finally one step
above that.

Recent events in the cloak-and-dagger business should have given all concerned clear warning that the *Pueblo* was being sent on a dangerous mission. Over the past ten years the Russians have made it quite clear that sniffing around their shores is hazardous. They have shot down U.S. airplanes on snooper flights outside their territorial waters over both the Norwegian Sea and Sea of Japan. They weren't even polite about this. They made no attempt to warn these planes—they just shot them down. In one case, they did have the courtesy to return our dead bodies to us.

Confronted with a *fait accompli* after the planes were shot down, we didn't see fit to make an issue of whether the planes were just inside or outside of territorial limits. We pulled our snoopers farther back and told them to keep their guns cocked and ready whenever they sighted Russian aircraft. There have been several exchanges of long-range gunfire since then, which haven't been publicized.

In the case of the U-2 flights, we definitely trespassed over Russian territory. But we flew so high that for a long time they couldn't reach us. They knew we were up there and tracked us by radar—but they never said a word. They waited till they could reach us with ground-to-air missiles, and then shot our plane down.

They still said nothing until they had booby-trapped us into some clumsy lying about it, and then they produced our pilot and the wreckage of his plane. So we quit flying U-2s over Russia. Now we do the same job with orbiting satellites and nothing is said. When the Russians put their Sputnik in orbit, it trespassed illegally over our territory several times a day, but we made no objection. International law is quite flexible in the snooping business and you go just as far as the other fellow will let you.

However, there are certain basic rules that all civilized

nations respect, even if they do stretch them at times. One is
that the high seas are free to everybody, and any naval vessel
has a right to go wherever it wants on them, even though there
is wide disagreement about where the high seas begin. We
claim they start at the three-mile limit. Many others, including
the North Koreans, claim a twelve-mile limit. Some claim
they begin at the edge of the continental shelf, often a hundred miles or more off shore. But the high seas, wherever they
begin, are supposed to be free—to snoopers as well as fishing
fleets, tramp steamers, or carrier task forces. This is why the
Russians, whenever they shoot down one of our planes, always
claim it was inside their territorial waters. This is why, in the
case of the *Pueblo,* the gooks wouldn't release our crew until
we signed a "confession" that the ship had invaded Korean
waters.

At any rate, no nation objects officially to electronic snooping. Everyone who can, does it. It just has to be done outside
territorial waters.

We got another stern warning that the snooper trade is
dangerous in the *Liberty* incident. The *Liberty* was another
converted merchant ship, somewhat bigger than the *Pueblo.*
She was obviously no conventional warship, but her array
of electronic antennas showed she was no Arab tramp steamer.
She was painted battleship gray and had big white numbers
on her bow. While outside territorial waters, and flying U.S.
colors, she was attacked without warning by Israeli planes
and PT boats. Unlike *Pueblo,* she fought back—as best she
could—and was able to limp away without being boarded.
Thirty-four of her crew were killed and seventy-five wounded.

The Israelis apologized and paid an indemnity for their
"mistake," which was indeed a stupid one for their Navy to
make. But this should have been plain warning to all concerned in the ELINT business that it was dangerous work. Ap-

parently this word never got to the *Pueblo* or to anyone in her chain of command, clear up to the very top.

Incidentally, there was a great difference in the way the fleet commanders reacted in the *Liberty* and *Pueblo* cases. When the *Liberty* called for help, Vice Admiral Martin of the Sixth Fleet started planes and ships to her assistance the instant he got her SOS. He didn't fiddle around asking anybody for authority to do so. He started help on the way and passed the word up the line, so they could stop him if they were too frightened by what might come of it.

In the *Pueblo* case, none of our ships or planes came anywhere near her. In one case we sent plenty of help, fast. In the other, we deserted our beleaguered ship.

In recent years, Russian snoopers have attached themselves to our fleets in both European and Asiatic waters. It is now SOP (Standard Operating Procedure) for their destroyers to hang around task groups of the Sixth and Seventh fleets. There is nothing illegal about this because the Russians have as much right under international law to be where they are as we have. Ordinary sea manners and naval courtesy require single ships to keep clear of ships in formation. But the Russians pay no attention to courtesy. In fact they often play chicken games with our ships, maneuvering into positions where they have the right of way under the rules of the road and forcing our ships to change course or fall out of formation to avoid collision. We have become accustomed to this, and it may have helped get us in the frame of mind that said, "these chicken games are annoying—but nothing will ever come of them."

Our other snooper ships have also been chevied and lured into chicken games. A sister ship of the *Pueblo* operating off the China and Korean coast had small craft crowd around it, zigzag across its bow, and make threatening gestures. But she

2

had never been actually molested. This, too, confirmed the general feeling prevailing all the way up the line that "it can't happen here." The JCS (Joint Chiefs of Staff) had actually been briefed weeks ahead of time on where the *Pueblo* was going and what she was going to do. After studying all angles on it, they had decided that it was a "minimal risk mission."

Finally, just before the *Pueblo* sailed on its last cruise, we had one more ominous warning that it might happen. The Koreans broadcast by radio that they would take drastic action against any future snooper ships that they found near their coast. Based on this broadcast, the NSA sent a warning to the JCS that *Pueblo's* mission might not be a "minimal risk" as the JCS had declared it to be. This warning was circulated on lower staff levels but never got to any of the chiefs. It was rerouted to CNO (Chief of Naval Operations) and CINCPAC, but didn't penetrate through their protective staffs either. As a result, the *Pueblo's* mission was officially "minimal risk" until the moment Bucher's signalman handed him the message from the gook subchaser: "Heave to, or I will fire."

Those who are familiar with Red tactics say they often bluster and make wild statements when accusing us of high crimes and misdemeanors, but that they seldom bluff when predicting what they intend to do. Be that as it may, in this case it was no bluff. But everybody except NSA thought it was.

From all the above incidents we should have known that the *Peublo* might get in trouble. We should have been ready to help her if she did. The simple fact is we were sound asleep. This is why, although you certainly can't condone Bucher's surrendering without a fight—you can't hang him for it either. Much bigger people than Bucher were caught flat-footed and refused to fight that day!

ELINT snooping is quite different from real spy work. A

spy knows that he will have all the resources of CIA behind him until he gets caught. Then he is disavowed, and the government denies any knowledge of him. This is well understood by everybody in the business.

An ELINT ship is an entirely different case. It is an official Navy ship, manned by members of the Armed Forces. Although it tries not to be conspicuous, it certainly operates openly. It cannot be disavowed; and, like any other Navy ship, it has a right to feel that if it gets in trouble and needs help, help will be forthcoming.

The seizure of the Pueblo was a flagrant act of piracy. One reason why we were caught so flat-footed is that civilized nations do not practice piracy any more. Since the War of 1812, the high seas have been free to the ships of all nations. Even if the *Pueblo* had entered Korean waters, which she had not— her seizure was still piracy, completely outside the bounds of international law.

But, of course, one of the handicaps we work under in dealing with the Communists is our respect for international law. We feel bound by the law of nations and by a decent regard for public opinion. The Communists are bound by nothing except their own self-interest.

The upshot of all this was that no one on the *Pueblo* had ever given serious thought to the idea that they might be boarded and captured. Apparently this possibility seemed as remote as that of the sky falling on them. The crew were not indoctrinated with the importance and danger of their job. No drills had ever been held on defending the ship or destroying her secret gear and scuttling.

The one big controlling fact in the *Pueblo* debacle is that no one could conceive of piracy as being an even remote possibility. A large number of supposedly smart men studied all angles of the *Pueblo*'s mission ahead of time, and all came to the same conclusion—it was a minimal risk. This big, top-level blunder overshadows all the others that were made in this tragedy of errors.

To understand the *Pueblo* affair, it is necessary to know how the Defense Department is organized and operates. Of course this changes from crisis to crisis and from one disaster to the next. But in general, there are two main lines of authority in the department; one over operations, the other over everything else.

For operations, the Army, Navy, Air Force, and Marines are all dumped into one pot and then split up into eight so-called unified commands. These are:

Alaskan Command
Atlantic Command
European Command
Pacific Command
Southern Command
Strike Command
SAC (Strategic Air Command)
Continental Air Defense Command

There are also major international commands under NATO. All the forces in each of these commands are under a single "unified" commander who gets his orders direct from the Secretary of Defense.

Until "Unification," right after World War II, the head of each of the military services was also the operational commander of that service, under the President. This is no longer true, although he is usually the whipping boy when anything goes wrong in his service, such as the *Liberty, Scorpion,* or *Pueblo* disasters. Fleet commanders now get their orders from the President through their unified commanders—not through the CNO.

The military heads of the Armed Forces are not even in the operational chain of command now, except indirectly as members of the Joint Chiefs of Staff. They are now responsible for the housekeeping and administration of their services —for their budget, training, equipment, and logistic support. Each service chief is a member of the JCS, who *advise* the Secretary, and at times the President, on operational matters.

In the pre-Unification Navy that I grew up in, the idea of full and inescapable responsibility for events at sea used to go a lot higher than the captain of a ship. As in any proper military organization, it went clear up the chain of command. Since the days of sail, an admiral's responsibility for the ships in his command was just as clear and as heavy as a captain's. It was an admiral's duty to see that no ship in his fleet was ever put in a spot where she might be lost without doing any good. When he sent a ship on detached duty, he saw to it that she was properly equipped to defend herself against all likely opposition, and he was prepared to get timely help to her if she needed it. When a ship was lost, everybody in the chain of command shared the blame, and had to be ready to justify whatever part he played in the operation. This was a basic fact of military life, and everyone knew it.

Since Unification, this is no longer true. Under the banner

of "Civilian Control of the Military," a bevy of assistant secretaries of defense and whiz kids have been taking over not only control, but also, command of the military. Dozens of bright-eyed young civilians who are experts in many fields except that of military operations have been meddling in the actual running of our fleets. One of the most shocking things about the *Pueblo* fiasco is that there is room for argument as to whether she was really under the command of the admirals in the Pacific Fleet or of the whiz kids in the Pentagon.

We are told, now, that the *Pueblo*'s next senior in the chain of command was Commander Naval Forces, Japan (Rear Admiral Johnson). This is a clear sign that there was something funny about *Pueblo*'s status. Normally, any Navy ship operating off the Korean coast would come under Commander, Seventh Fleet. All other ships in that area did, and the only help the Navy could send to the *Pueblo* would have to come from the Seventh Fleet. Commander Naval Forces, Japan is a housekeeping shore job that runs our naval bases and small craft in Japan. The only real ship he had under his command was the U.S.S. *Pueblo,* and in her case, "command" was purely nominal. As soon as the *Pueblo* got in trouble, the whole can of worms was dumped in the lap of Commander in Chief, Pacific.

The actual command status of the ship was foggy. She was in the bailiwick of Commander in Chief Pacific (Admiral Sharp), but she was not really a part of the Pacific Fleet. Responsibility for her and authority over her were divided, and as is always the case when disaster strikes, everyone concerned can now blame it on everyone else.

As a matter of Pentagon politics, the Navy may have to take the rap for the *Pueblo.* The case is somewhat like the Bay of Pigs, where everybody had a piece of the action until the stuff hit the fan, and then President Kennedy had to accept full responsibility.

This sad state of elusive responsibility results from a process that has been going on in the Pentagon ever since Forrestal left office as the first Secretary of Defense. Operational control of far-flung military units is being taken over by Sec Def and his many undersecretaries and special assistants, otherwise known as whiz kids. Commanders of military units on the other side of the earth get orders direct from the Pentagon bypassing normal command channels.

This is done in the name of Civilian Control of the Military, which has become a sacred cow since Unification. Civilian *control* is essential under our form of government—and we've always had it, since the Commander in Chief was always the President. F.D.R. exercised his control by firing Admiral Kimmel and General Short right after Pearl Harbor. He also exercised it when he appointed Admiral Ernie King COMINCH and CNO. He still had *control*, even with a tough character like Uncle Ernie running the Navy, because Admiral King obeyed all policy directives he got from the President and passed them along through proper naval channels to be carried out. But if the President or anyone else had tried to bypass Admiral King and take command of any of his fleets, F.D.R. would have had to get himself a new COMINCH and CNO real fast.

President Truman certainly exercised civilian *control* when he fired General MacArthur. So did Secretary of Defense Louis Johnson when he canned Admiral Denfield as CNO, and Mr. McNamara when he sacked Admiral George Anderson.

It seems strange that we raise such a fuss about civilian control of the military and keep putting men in the White House to run the whole show who are ex-military men.

Every President we have had since Hoover has been tarred with the military brush.

The Navy, of course, claims F.D.R. as one of its own, since he was Assistant Secretary of the Navy in World War I. In some ways he was "more Catholic than the Pope." President Truman was a battery commander in that war. General Eisenhower was a West Pointer and lifetime career officer. And presidents Kennedy, Johnson, and Nixon are all ex-Navy men. Fortunately, these men with military experience know there are two sides to this question of control.

Command and control are two different things, and when we mix them, as we are doing now, we court disaster. Generals and admirals on the firing line who have fought in many bloody battles now have to ask the Pentagon for permission to do things that local knowledge and battle experience tell them must be done. The answer often comes back from some smart young whiz kid who was in grade school during World War II and has never been in even an alley fight.

This handcuffing of commanders in the field and concentrating power to act in the Pentagon reached its high point under the regime of Mr. McNamara and his band of starry-eyed "experts." Under the banners of Cost Effectiveness and Civilian Control of the Military, they have changed the Defense Department from a military headquarters to the great front office of a corporate business institution.

If we can believe the figures put out by its computers and press agents, the Defense Department now spends its lion's share of the national budget in a very scientific manner. The mechanical brains grind out arrays of figures showing that the whiz kids are saving the taxpayers billions and billions of dollars every year, even though while they are doing it, the defense budget keeps inflating until the balloon is bursting at the seams. Their cost effectiveness studies show that the

TFX airplane contract was a masterpiece of scientific management. Admiral George Anderson, who was CNO at this time, challenged these studies and said the TFX would never be a good Navy airplane. This caused Mr. McNamara to exercise his civilian control and sack Admiral Anderson. When these studies took shape in metal airplanes, a series of resounding crashes showed that some young expert had punched the wrong buttons on his computer, and Admiral Anderson was right.

But even if all the Defense Department's claims about scientific management and business efficiency were true, the fact still is that the department and its computers cannot do a proper job of defending the country. The *Pueblo* fiasco is a small but ominous example of what has gone wrong. Civilian control? Certainly. Command? No.

Civilian control has merit when applied to the business functions of the Pentagon in spending its sixty-billion-dollar chunk of the national budget. Scientific management is certainly needed in awarding huge national contracts to the defense industry, in channeling research and development, in controlling the inventory of military supplies, and in simply keeping the books straight in a department that has such a great effect on the economy of the whole country.

Perhaps whiz kids and computers can do a better job in these areas than generals and admirals, who spend most of their lives trying to learn how to use the products of all this effort. But McNamara and his band were not satisfied to stick to this area. They do control the purse strings, and their computers do a fairly good job, despite such bloopers as the TFX and refusal to build nuclear-powered ships. But they have also usurped military command of the operating forces.

Admiral Anderson was finally sacked because he wouldn't lie to Congress when they pinned him down on his opinion about the TFX. But his troubles with Mr. McNamara began before that. During the Cuban missile crisis Mr. McNamara and several public relations types came into the CNO operations room one night to see what was happening around Cuba. As they studied the big operations display board, McNamara noticed that one destroyer was unsymetrically placed with respect to the others in the blockade line. He asked Anderson, "Why?"

The destroyer was doing a job that Anderson did not want noised about the corridors of the Pentagon—or anywhere else in Washington. He gave a noncommittal answer. McNamara insisted on further details, thus focusing the attention of all present on this ship. When Anderson again gave an evasive answer, tempers began to rise and finally, Anderson had to ask McNamara to step into a private cubbyhole, where he told him this ship was sitting on top of a Russian submarine. McNamara resented this incident, and his public relations people leaked it as evidence of a rebellious attitude on Admiral Anderson's part.

In a typical *reductio ad absurdum,* military command is now taken over by civilian assistant secretaries of defense, while administration and logistic support is relegated to the service chiefs. The Chiefs of Staff of the Army and Air Force and the CNO are the military heads of the services. But they are not even in the military chain of command, which now runs direct from Sec Def to the unified commanders in the field.

True, the service chiefs get into the act in an advisory role, because they are also the Joint Chiefs of Staff. But even the JCS have been downgraded by the McNamara regime to mere figureheads. Much of the Joint Chiefs' proper business of giving broad strategic advice is now farmed out to civilian think factories, which speak the whiz kids' language better than the Joint Chiefs do.

This results in the anomaly of CINCPAC looking to his military chief, CNO, for beans, bullets, and logistic support, but to Sec Def and the whiz kids for military direction.

The miracle of modern communications gives the experts in the Pentagon ivory tower a false sense of being able to be right on top of events anywhere in the world. Side-band radio, satellite relay stations, and other things make it possible for them to talk directly to any point on the globe. Sec Def can tell his aide, "Get me the skipper of the *Pueblo* on the horn," and within a few minutes, he can be talking to the *Pueblo* in the Sea of Japan. When a call originates in Sec Def's office, it has a great deal of horsepower behind it and takes precedence over all other traffic. Other important messages are cut off in the middle of a word; channels are cleared, and special channels set up fast. Sec Def's call gets through in a hurry.

But it doesn't work that way for the skipper of the *Pueblo!* If he makes a message "CRITIC," it means, "for the attention of the White House." But the message has to go through a half-dozen HQs on the way to the White House, and in each one, a duty officer has to find his boss and convince him that the skipper of the *Pueblo* is justified in using CRITIC before he fires it up the line. In Washington, somebody has to decide to wake up the President from a sound sleep—and this isn't done by a mess boy! All this takes time —so much time that before the President gets the word, the battle may be over. In the case of the *Pueblo*, by the time the President learned she was being boarded by pirates, it was too late for him to do anything.

Actually, when Bucher first realized he might be in trouble, the day before the capture, his report of this fact took fourteen hours to get to the next senior in his chain of command, Rear Admiral Johnson in Yokosuka. This is a scandal to the jaybirds, and heads should roll on account of it. But it shows that this instant communication doesn't work both ways. On the day of the capture, from the time Bucher realized he was in bad trouble until his ship was in enemy hands was about one hour and three quarters. From the time he sent his SOS "CRITIC" until the National Communication Center in Washington got it was two hours and a half. How long it took to get to the White House has never been publicly admitted.

Someone in the chain of command should have stuck his neck out and taken action on his own hook. Actually, Commander Seventh Fleet did start ships on the way to the Sea of Japan as soon as he got *Pueblo*'s SOS. But he wouldn't send planes on his own authority and no one ever told him to. He could have had overwhelming force in Wonsan the next day, but he also had to have orders from higher authority to do that. They never came.

Much Pentagon gobbledegook has been put out since to explain why. They say that any attempt by us to either rescue or destroy the ship would have resulted in the death of her crew. At the Navy inquiry, the *Pueblo* crew members said they fully expected us to retaliate for their capture—and hoped we would, regardless of how it affected their fate. They were willing to die if we did, and were shocked and disillusioned when we didn't.

This, of course, is just a flagrant example of the submissive philosophy which is now infecting our whole country: "Don't get involved trying to stop evil—somebody might get hurt."

An atomic war would be so disastrous for the country and the rest of the world that action on any incident that might escalate into a big war is always referred to the President.

Since China is now becoming an atomic power and the Russians are in cahoots with all enemies of the United States, almost any bit of international violence anywhere in the world has the possibility of escalating. So authority to take action in cases like the *Pueblo* is being concentrated more and more in the White House.

If the local commanders had responded to the *Pueblo's* SOS with prompt and adequate force, there is a good chance the gooks would have put their tails between their legs and run. The worst that might have happened would have been to sink the ship and lose the crew. It is absurd to say this might have escalated into a big war—unless we wanted one. It takes two to escalate. After either rescuing or recovering the ship, we would simply withdraw, and then it would be the "adversary's" move. In this case, the adversaries had no way of waging a big war, and it's ridiculous to think the Russians would have done it for them.

And even if a rescue had threatened to escalate into something big, we could always squirm out of it if we got scared badly enough. We could disavow and fire the military officers who did it, apologize, and give the ship back to the gooks.

Don't brush this idea off as being absurd. It is no more so than the abject apology we made to the gooks a year later to get our men back.

The danger of escalating a minor incident has led to the framing of so-called rules of engagement. These attempt to say how far a ship or plane can go in defending itself against hostile action—and how far local commanders can go on their own authority in supporting their forces if attacked.

These rules are very difficult to write, because they are meant to guide low-level officers in making high-level decisions when their lives may be at stake. They have to cover an almost infinite range of situations, and one that they didn't foresee was piracy in the year of 1968.

There is, of course, no question that *Pueblo* had a right to defend herself and repel boarders. The commanders of the Fifth Air Force and the Seventh Fleet apparently had the right to defend her up to a certain point under the so-called doctrine of hot pursuit. This means that if they started shooting on the high seas, they could continue the action some indefinite distance inside territorial waters. But once the action was broken off or the *Pueblo* got into Wonsan Harbor, action against her then became retaliation and required approval from Washington.

The doctrine of hot pursuit goes back to the days of sail. In prohibition days the Coast Guard applied it to booze smugglers off our coasts. Rum runners were free to hang around our coasts outside the three-mile limit. But if the Coast Guard caught them inside the three-mile limit, it could board and capture them. Under the doctrine of hot pursuit, if the Coast Guard spotted them inside the three-mile limit but they got outside before the Coast Guard overhauled them, they were still eligible for capture. We turn this doctrine around now and say that if piracy is committed on the high seas, we can continue the pursuit of pirates inside territorial waters.

Admiral Sharp, in discussing these rules before the House Armed Services Committee, admitted that the rules are fuzzy, need overhauling, and that rewriting them is a very difficult job. He declined to discuss this any further in open session because the rules are—and should be—classified. We certainly can't afford to tell the "adversary" ahead of time just how far he can go before we will react.

But current policy requires that an incident that can escalate be referred to the White House. And despite the miracle of modern communications, it takes time for a message going *up* the chain of command to penetrate the barriers and get to the White House. By the time *Pueblo*'s SOS got there, it was all over. What should have been an unsuccessful attempt at piracy had become a smashing success for a bunch of irresponsible savages. Instead of blowing over in a few days, it dragged out into a year of torture for our men and humiliation for the United States. This is one of the prices we pay for our massive retaliation weapons—so massive that we can't use them!

So the big reason why we did nothing to help the *Pueblo* is that we just didn't have the guts to. There were other reasons too. When Rear Admiral Johnson got *Pueblo*'s SOS, he immediately *requested* help from the Fifth Air Force in Japan and from the Seventh Fleet. However, there were difficulties.

Under the treaty that gives us bases in Japan, we cannot launch offensive missions from these bases. Strict adherence to this treaty eliminated the use of Marine or Air Force planes based in Japan, four hundred miles from Wonsan.

The Fifth Air Force had planes in South Korea, only a few minutes' flight from Wonsan, but they were armed with atom bombs. To remove the bombs and rearm them would take too long.

The nearest base from which the Air Force could send any planes was Okinawa, seven hundred miles away. Since they had not been asked to stand by for such a mission, it required two hours and forty minutes to launch a strike.

The nearest planes in the Seventh Fleet were on the *Enterprise*, five hundred miles to the south of Wonsan. Why she couldn't launch planes quickly to land and refuel, if necessary, in South Korea—I don't know. But she didn't.

The South Koreans had planes that might have got there

very quickly, but we wouldn't ask for them. When the question, "Why?" was asked at the Armed Services Committee hearing, the Navy immediately requested executive session.

Incidentally, the Navy had a bad time at the House Armed Services Committee hearings over what items were still classified after the gooks got our whole ship. Whenever the going got tough, the Navy would ask for executive session. I don't blame them one bit for this, because some pretty gawd-awful bloopers were being aired.

The committee finally got fed up with this. At one point, a document called Pink Root Instructions came up for discussion, and the Navy said it would have to be in executive session because the paper was highly classified by both Navy and NSA. A member of the committee then held up a sheaf of papers and said, "I have the text of it here, as broadcast on February 18, 1968, with no classification, from Pyongyang!"

The simple fact is that we had no planes whatever earmarked to support the *Pueblo*. We just stuck her out on the end of a long limb and left her there. This is inexcusable, because in this day and age we have so-called contingency plans to cover almost everything that can come up. The planning section of every operational staff is supposed to dream up possible contingencies that may arise in their area and to have detailed plans made up and ready to execute in case their nightmares come true. They cover such things as another Berlin blockade, revolutions in the Caribbean and Central America, closing off the Suez Canal, riots in our big cities, and the March on the Pentagon. These plans are supposed to cover all details that can be foreseen: forces available, task organization, command channels, logistics, and manner of placing the plan in operation.

In the case of the *Pueblo*, no plan whatever had been

drawn up to help her because she belonged to the ivory tower in the Pentagon. Another reason is, of course, that piracy on the high seas is a very unlikely contingency. The last experience we had with it was back in 1815, when Stephen Decatur cleaned out the Barbary pirates in the Mediterranean. But, past events had given us plenty of warning that she might be harassed, and some sort of provision should have been made to chase off her hecklers, even if no one could reasonably be expected to foresee the possibility of boarding and capture.

Even at this late date, it is difficult for us to get it through our heads that the Communists are capable of *anything*, no matter how fantastic it seems.

The voyage on which *Pueblo* was captured was her first mission as an ELINT ship, and the first such job for nearly everyone on board. Before sailing, Bucher was thoroughly briefed by the skipper of the *Banner*, a similar ship that had made sixteen such missions and had just returned from Korean waters.

The *Banner's* skipper told of many brushes with small craft, which joined up on him and hung around making a nuisance of themselves. They would circle around him close aboard, sniff around his stern, and zigzag across his bow. They played chicken games with him and maneuvered to get him into situations where they had the right of way under international rules of the road and he'd had to change course to avoid collision. The Russians had been doing this in the Mediterranean, too, and CNO had recently put out a directive warning our skippers about it, and telling them to follow rules of the road, but not to be intimidated. The *Banner's* skipper told Bucher the gooks had heckled and chevied him and shown very bad sea manners, but had not actually molested him. They had annoyed him, but not worried him.

The *Banner*'s skipper also told about usually having trouble getting anyone to answer when he decided to break radio silence. Bucher conferred with the CO of the Navy radio station in Japan about this, and tried to impress him with the importance of reliable radio communications. He was given a tale of woe about technical difficulties in that area, and left the conference unhappy.

Bucher also had several sessions with Rear Admiral Johnson, who would be his OTC (Officer in Tactical Command) on this mission. Johnson told him to be careful not to antagonize any North Korean hecklers and to keep the canvas covers on his two 50-caliber machine guns unless a dire emergency required their removal. Bucher asked if he could use the guns to repel boarders and Johnson told him "yes," but that he was "quite sure the guns would never be needed."

The upshot of all this was that when Bucher sailed, he felt the biggest danger he faced was getting maneuvered into a collision in which the "adversary" had the right of way under international rules of the road.

Bucher had not been told that the Koreans had broadcast a radio threat to take drastic action against the next snooper ship they saw. Perhaps our intelligence people considered this info too highly classified to pass on to Bucher!

The *Pueblo* sailed from Sasebo, Japan, on January 11, 1968. Her operating area was on the other side of the Sea of Japan, only four hundred miles from the Japanese main islands. Her sailing order was written by Rear Admiral Johnson (see Appendix C) and told her to gather electronic intelligence to be analyzed by experts back in Washington, and also to get oceanographic data on sea water temperature, salinity, depths, and currents.

She was directed to stay more than thirteen miles offshore. The United States holds that territorial waters only extend three miles out from shore. But the Koreans claim a twelve-mile limit, and *Pueblo* was told to stay outside of it. Thirteen miles out she would be on the high seas, which all civilized nations have recognized for centuries as being free to everybody.

The sailing order specifically warned Bucher to keep his guns covered except "where threat to survival is obvious."

Pueblo arrived on station sixteen miles off the Korean coast on January 21, expecting to work along the coast outside the twelve-mile limit for about five days. Her crew had had no drills in the use of her guns, in scuttling, or in destroying her black boxes and secret papers. There were ten hand-held Thompson submachine guns aboard, but no plans had been made to use them in repelling boarders.

At noon on January 22, *Pueblo* was lying to about sixteen miles from the nearest land, twenty miles from Wonsan, when two "fishing" vessels began circling her. Although these craft looked like fishermen, their actions soon indicated they were not. They circled *Pueblo* close aboard with their crews looking her over carefully through binoculars and taking photographs.

Bucher hoisted a signal saying he was engaged in oceanographic work. After they had hung around for sometime, he decided to break radio silence and report to Rear Admiral Johnson that he was being shadowed.

It took fourteen hours to establish communication with Navy radio Japan. This is scandalous, and confirmed Bucher's misgivings at his conference before sailing. Contact should have been almost instantaneous. This was like finding the only nearby fire alarm box locked when your house is burning.

Bucher's report simply said he had been detected, was being shadowed, and caused no alarm when it finally did get through to Johnson's HQ. There was no reason why it should. But the fourteen-hour delay in transmission should have caused some communicators' heads to roll. Apparently it didn't.

Next morning about eleven o'clock *Pueblo* finally got a two-way teletype circuit working with Japan and sent the SITREP (Situation Report) on being discovered. They followed this with a number of routine reports on the technical data they had been gathering. Before they were finished, other things began to happen around them, and Bucher told his radiomen to hold the circuit open. For the next three and one half hours, the circuit was kept alive and there was firm radio contact between *Pueblo* and Japan.

About noon when *Pueblo* was dead in the water near the same position as the day before, a subchaser flying the North Korean flag came over the horizon at high speed. The subchaser closed to half a mile and began circling the *Pueblo* with her guns manned and trained on her. Bucher could see men on deck with submachine guns and rifles. He checked his position by radar and found he was sixteen miles from nearest land, well outside territorial waters.

Most of *Pueblo*'s crew were below decks out of sight. Those on deck were not in naval uniform, and *Pueblo* had no colors flying. The canvas covers were on her machine guns and were heavily coated with ice.

In a few minutes the subchaser ran up the international signal flags saying, "What is your nationality?"

Bucher responded by hoisting U.S. colors. He also called the engine room and told them, "Stand by to answer bells."

The next flag hoist from the subchaser was an ominous one. It said, "Heave to, or I will fire."

This didn't make much sense because *Pueblo* was already hove to and dead in the water. Bucher says his first reaction to it was that it was just stupidity in picking the wrong signal from the international code book. But taking it at its face value, and in response to hoisting U.S. colors, it did show that maybe more than the normal heckling might be afoot.

Bucher hoisted a signal saying, "I am in international waters," and cracked off a radio to Japan headed "CRITIC," which means "for White House attention." In it he reported the threat to fire on him but said he thought they were just trying to intimidate him, and he intended to stay in the area if practicable. The time was 1252 local—0352 Zed.

To keep the teletype circuit hot, for the next two and one half hours the radio operators in *Pueblo* and Japan exchanged unofficial chatter, between official messages. Looking at this chatter now, it is obvious the *Pueblo*'s operators were worried about what was going on around them. (See Appendix D)

The official messages that Bucher sent indicate concern, too, but more by the high classification he gave them and the top-level addresses than by their actual wording. From noon until 1330, the few messages that Bucher sent indicated severe harassment, but nothing worse than the *Banner* had been subjected to before him. Although soon after noon he became concerned enough to discuss scuttling with his chief engineer, his messages were factual and didn't cause any alarm at the other end. No Navy skipper likes to send a message to his boss saying, "I'm scared," and Bucher didn't for some time. So nobody in Japan got excited about what was happening.

Soon after the "heave to" signal, three PT boats came boiling over the horizon and began circling *Pueblo* with their

guns manned and trained on her. This was when Bucher
sent for his engineer and discussed the possibility of scuttling.
The engineer said it would take two and one half hours to
scuttle and pointed out that they were in shallow water
(180 feet) where divers would have no trouble reaching her
on the bottom. They agreed that scuttling was impractical.

This requires explanation. If any thought had been given
to scuttling ahead of time and proper plans had been made,
it should have been possible to sink the ship in perhaps fifteen
minutes—even without the explosives Bucher had requested
and been denied. The shallow water was of little importance.
If *Pueblo* had been scuttled sixteen miles offshore, there
could have been no quibbling about her being in international
waters. We would have had a perfect right to move in with
whatever force might be necessary and to send our own
divers down to recover whatever we wanted from her.

And even if they couldn't scuttle or blow her up, they
could have set fire to her and destroyed her. The crew
would have to go overboard in either case, and couldn't be
sure that the Koreans would rescue them. But that was a
risk, not a certainty. Soldiers are required to take risks every
day to protect the interests of the United States. The Koreans
would be almost certain to rescue them, because live Americans are valuable hostages.

There are other things which Bucher could have done when
it became apparent they were going to try to board him. He
could have crippled his main engines. He could have let go
his anchors and disabled his anchor engine so they couldn't
be raised. He could have jammed his rudder hard over and
disabled his rudder engine. True, the gooks could have slipped
the anchor cables. But this would take time. And towing
Pueblo in with her rudder hard over would also have taken
time. These two things together could have delayed *Pueblo*'s

arrival in Wonsan by quite a few hours. This would have been a little less humiliating than having her steam right in under her own power.

Right after the scuttling discussion, one of the circling PT boats came close aboard and began backing down, with armed men on deck who looked like they meant to board. Meantime, another subchaser and PT boat had showed up, and two MIGs were circling overhead. Bucher decided it was time to get out of there. He hoisted a signal, "Thank you for your courtesy—am departing," and went ahead at 5 knots, heading for the open sea, thus stopping the attempt to board. He got off another CRITIC message telling of the boarding attempt and saying he was departing the area, time group 0415 ZED (1315 local time).

The PT boats closed in. Two took station close astern, and two began porpoising across the bow. The MIGs were circling overhead. One subchaser again hoisted the signal, "Heave to, or I will fire."

Bucher continued moving seaward at 5 knots and passed the word, "Stand by to destroy confidential papers." This word got to his own crew proper, but didn't penetrate to the communicators' holy of holies where all the really secret stuff was. At this point, Bucher was certainly concerned for the safety of his ship—as indicated by this order. But he still didn't realize that this was *it*.

Suddenly, at about 1330, the gook SC opened fire with its 57-mm. cannon, knocking out some of *Pueblo*'s radio antennas and wounding Bucher and two of his men on the bridge with their first shots. In one shattering split second, the incident changed from harassment to piracy, and time was turned back 150 years.

Bucher picked himself up off the deck bleeding from a splinter wound and passed the word, "Destroy secret papers."

3

This time, the word penetrated to the inner sanctum. Bucher stopped his engines and the gooks ceased fire.

The operators' chatter had been keeping Japan informed as to what was happening, and by now it told them things were getting pretty desperate. It was now quite clear that this was no mere heckling incident, and that the gooks meant to board and capture the ship. Bucher still had his guns covered, and the canvas covers were caked with ice.

Bucher's sailing orders said to keep his guns covered. This was a stupid order, like telling an ostrich to keep its head buried in the sand. But stupid orders get issued in large organizations, including even the Navy sometimes, and subordinates must obey them—*up to a point.*

But there comes a time when it is an officer's duty to disobey a stupid order. This point is reached when the basis on which the order was issued is no longer valid. This happened at the Battle of Copenhagen, when the senior British admiral hoisted a signal telling Admiral Nelson to do something foolish. Nelson put his telescope to his blind eye and said, "I can't see the signal." This point was reached for Bucher when the SC signaled, "Heave to, or I will fire," an hour before. In fact, for most officers it would have been reached twenty-four hours before that—when the gook fishing vessels began shadowing.

The order to keep his guns covered was obviously based on the assumption that no one would ever try to board. As soon as there was any doubt about this, Bucher should have disobeyed the order and unlimbered his guns.

Press reports say he testified it would have taken an hour to break the ice and get the covers off. I can't believe he said that. A pair of husky sailors could have ripped them off in one minute.

This matter of disobeying orders is a delicate one. It's a

good idea to be sure you are right when you do it—and there are certain orders that are absolute and can never be disobeyed. The orders to a Polaris sub skipper, for example. Under no circumstances whatever can he fire his missiles on his own hook, or refuse to fire when he gets an order from the President to do so. If he has any qualms whatever about blind obedience in this matter, he has no right to accept command of a Polaris sub.

But an order to keep your guns covered is not one of the absolute ones. Bucher should have disobeyed it an hour and a half earlier. If anyone had questioned this later, his answer was easy: "I was there, Bud, and I thought the safety of my ship required it." One of the penalties you pay for the privilege of command is the duty to make decisions of this kind.

After they fired on him Bucher had another big command decision to make—fight or surrender? This wasn't a decision that he had mulled over ahead of time, considering all the angles. Up to the moment they opened up on him, he didn't think they really meant to do any more than harass him as they had the *Banner*. Then, suddenly, it was a completely new ball game and all previous rules were down the drain. We can argue for hours, now, about all the things he might have done, and how they might have turned out. But Bucher had to make up his mind then and there.

Two things determined his decisions. In order of importance, they were: (1) saving the lives of his men; (2) keeping control of his ship as long as possible to destroy as many of his secret papers as he could. He decided not to fight, but to stall for time and delay losing control of the ship as long as possible. He had the word passed on the loud speakers, "If captured, give only name, rank, serial number, and date of birth."

At this time (1330) the "unofficial" radio chatter said, "We are being boarded. We are being boarded. SOS. SOS . . ." repeated thirteen times. This was a little premature, because the boarders didn't get aboard for another hour. Later, when the Navy Department was trying to alibi for failing to rescue *Pueblo*, it classified this message as "radio operator chatter." The Department claimed that Bucher failed to send proper official messages.

However, in the Navy I grew up in an SOS, repeated thirteen times was treated as about the most official message a ship could send. It didn't make a damn bit of difference who sent it.

At 1400, the SC sent, "Follow me. I have a pilot." Bucher fell in astern of the SC, proceeding at his lowest speed of 5 knots. When the gooks demanded more speed, he played dumb and indicated that was the best he could do. Bucher went down to the communications center at this time and was shocked to see how much secret stuff they had piled on the deck and how slow the destruction was going. While there he dictated the following to the radioman ". . . have been requested to follow in to Wonsan. Have three wounded and one man with leg blown off. Have not used weapons or uncovered 50 caliber. Destroying all key lists and as much electronic equipment as possible. How about some help. These guys mean business. Have sustained small wound in rectum. Do not intend to offer any resistance . . . do not know if communication spaces will be entered." The time of this message was around 1400. Admiral Johnson's HQ in Japan had finally hit the panic button about 1330 and by now, everything on the *Pueblo* circuit, including the chatter, was on its way up the whole chain of command. This was an hour and a half after the message, "Heave to, or I will fire" had been relayed to Japan.

This message was also classified as "operator chatter" by the Navy Department, perhaps because it didn't have an official time-date group on it. This is more pettifogging. The whole nature of the message shows that it came from the captain himself—even apart from the intimate personal details as to the location of his wound.

Bucher went back to the bridge and kept tagging along slowly astern of the SC. He had sent an SOS and a CRITIC message over an hour ago. Japan was only four hundred miles away. South Korea, where the United States had air bases and planes, was just over the horizon fifty miles to the south. Help might be arriving any minute. By tagging along slowly, he might retain internal control of his ship 'til help arrived.

He made another trip to the communications room, found the deck still piled with papers and the men trying to smash the black boxes with fire axes and sledge hammers. Lieutenant Harris informed him they were not going to be able to destroy all papers and had so notified Japan.

Bucher returned to the bridge, picking up his Navy cap from his room on the way there to replace the ski cap he had been wearing. If he had to greet visitors coming aboard, he wanted to do it wearing a proper cap!

Back on the bridge, he ordered the engines to slow down and stop—hoping to gain time for destroying things. This immediately brought a blast of gunfire which drove everyone off the bridge and into the pilothouse. On the way down from the bridge, bullets smacked into the bulkhead on both sides of Bucher, inches away. In the pilothouse he rang up slow ahead again to the engines.

This was at about 1430. Within five minutes, a PT boat pulled up astern and threw a line aboard the *Pueblo*. *Someone on board secured it for them* (!) and a party of eight or ten armed men scrambled aboard and took possession of *Pueblo*. We had eighty-three men aboard *Pueblo*, ten Thompson submachine guns, and seven 45-caliber pistols. The ten gooks met no resistance.

That small boarding party had every reason to expect they would be greeted by a blast of gunfire and killed. If they had reasoned the way we did, they would have said, "No. It's too dangerous. We won't go aboard." But they don't reason that way. They swarmed aboard and found, to their amazement, that they had eighty-two submissive prisoners on their hands.

It behooves us to give serious thought to this. If preservation of life is the main objective of our Armed Forces, we can achieve it very easily at the price of surrender. We will also wind up as a satellite nation of some country whose soldiers are not afraid to risk dying for it.

Anyway, the gooks got aboard and took over. *Pueblo*'s last transmission at about 1432 was, "Being boarded at this time. Four men injured, one critically. Going off the air now and destroying this gear."

Two guards stayed with Bucher and the helmsman in the pilothouse, two took station in the engine room where two of our men continued to operate the engines, and the other four or six herded the *Pueblo*'s remaining seventy-eight men together on the stern. There they made them kneel, and cuffed and beat them while they hog-tied and blindfolded them.

The picture presented here is an incredible one: seventy-nine Americans meekly submitting to a half-dozen gooks! Never before in our history had such a thing happened. Bucher said later at the court of inquiry that the thought occurred to him that if our planes showed up, his men might overpower the guards and take the ship back, and that he was prepared to pass the word for this if planes did come. He should have thought of that an hour earlier!

Half an hour later, around three o'clock, more gooks came aboard, including a colonel whom Bucher calls the Scar. The Scar had Bucher show him around the ship, urging him along with kicks and blows. He asked a lot of questions to which Bucher gave evasive answers. When they came to the incinerator, Bucher said they used it for making ice cream, and got a crack on the head with a pistol butt for it.

A pilot had come aboard with the Scar and took over the steering from Bucher's helmsman. The pilot rang up full speed, and Bucher's men in the engine room obediently revved the engines up to 12½ knots. At about a quarter to five, *Pueblo* was abeam of Ung Do island, ten miles from Wonsan. It wasn't dark for another hour and twenty minutes —at 6:06 P.M. Pueblo tied up to the dock in Wonsan at eight-thirty, and a gaggle of gook generals and admirals came aboard to gloat over their prize.

Our men were then paraded in chains before jeering spitting mobs in Wonsan and hauled off to a prison camp for humiliation, abuse, and torture.

So there is the story of events off Wonsan on the afternoon of January 23, 1968. What happened on board *Pueblo* between noon and 8 P.M. that day has been well covered by the Navy court of inquiry—most of it in public session. It is a heart-rending story that generates great sympathy for the men involved. But it's impossible to make anything heroic out of it. There is a lot more to the story that should be aired, and probably will be by Congress. But before taking up any of these other matters, let's see how Commander Bucher comes out of the events just described.

Since long before Columbus' time the captain of a ship has had almost unlimited authority over all on board his ship and absolute responsibility for the ship. If a ship is lucky and does something good, the captain is entitled to be smugly modest in accepting credit for it—even if he was sound asleep in his bunk when it happened. By the same token, if something bad happens to the ship, the captain gets the blame, even though he may have had no control over the events in question. The captain is supposed to *have* control. This is just one of the facts of life at sea, accepted by all seafaring men.

Because of this fact, if you listen to a group of officers discussing events at sea, you can usually pick out the skippers, just from the pronouns they use. Non-skippers will say "we" when speaking of what their own ship did, or "she" when telling what another ship did. Captains say, "I did so and so—" and, "he" when speaking of the other ship. This isn't due to egotism. It simply reflects the fact that the captain is responsible for whatever the ship does.

In any ordinary ship, the captain cannot escape responsibility for everything on board his ship. On the *Pueblo*, responsibility was fuzzy in one important area, the electronic snooping department. Bucher had no real need to know all the details of the black chamber activities that went on there and was not cleared for knowledge of them. As a rule he stayed out of that area and let Lieutenant Harris run the show. However, when the moment of truth came, he realized he was holding the sack for the snoopers as well as for the rest of the ship.

In the old days before radio, a skipper was on his own as soon as the land dropped out of sight astern. The captain of a U.S. man-o'-war often had to take action on his own hook that committed the country in high-level international affairs. Radio has tied skippers to the apron strings of the high-level officials in Washington.

But, as Bucher found out that afternoon off Wonsan, despite the miracles of radio, there can still come a time when the captain has to take immediate and important action on his authority alone. Time can be turned back, and a skipper may have to make a life or death decision quickly and on his own—just as in the days of sail.

There is only one stand the Navy can take about Bucher's decision to surrender without a fight. It was wrong. It violated tradition, the Code of Conduct, and the Navy Regulations.

As will be seen next there were many others who failed in their duty to the United States that afternoon, all much senior to Bucher. But this doesn't excuse his failure. Even when his superiors let him down the captain is still bound to repel boarders from his ship.

So much for events aboard *Pueblo* that afternoon. It is a humiliating story. But what happened all the way up the chain of command that day—or more accurately, what *didn't* happen —is even more humiliating. Radio messages flew halfway around the world at the speed of light. Top officials of the government were routed out of their beds in the middle of the night, and hurried down to the White House for a top-secret conference in the war room. But absolutely nothing happened until almost a year later, when the United States signed a false confession that *Pueblo* had intruded on Korean territorial waters and made an abject apology for it.

Quite possibly the full story of the high-level futility that night will not be revealed for some time. Most of it is now classified as top secret—essential to the national defense. I fully agree with this classification because a public airing of the whole sorry mess might do grave injury to the national defense. It might expose incompetence in very high places and shake public confidence in our whole system of government.

Of course it is bound to leak out eventually, when those who were in on it get ready to write their memoirs. When those who helped to make the blunders that day find a publisher who wants to bring out a book revealing all, they will find reason for declassifying this top-secret info.

What follows in this book is not based on any leaks from inside sources. Most of it comes from the public record of the Navy court of inquiry and from Congressional hearings. The rest is an educated guess by one who spent a lifetime in the Navy, the latter part of it in top-level circles around the Pentagon, and who knows how things happen there. These guesses are at least as apt to be right as the "revelations" which may later be made by top-level memoir writers who won't tell the whole story—only the parts that don't make them look too bad.

Before following the action up the chain of command from *Pueblo* to the White House, we must say a word about time. The Sea of Japan and Washington are on opposite sides of the earth and on different sides of the international date line. Between Washington and Wonsan, there is a difference of ten or fourteen hours, depending on how you look at it. Wonsan and Tokyo are in time zone plus 9, Honolulu is in time zone minus 10, and Washington is in time zone minus 5. Time zones are numbered, of course, from Greenwich, England, where longitude begins.

To keep time straight in the Navy's world-wide communications system, radio operators put a six-digit number at the beginning of each message they transmit. The first two digits are the date and the next four are the Greenwich Civil Time by a twenty-four-hour clock. This is known as Zed Time, and clocks keeping Zed Time read the same all over the world at any given instant of time. Thus, messages bearing the time group 230352 Zed were written at the same time, no matter where they came from, what the local time was there, or how long they were delayed in transmission. The time group on *Pueblo's* first call for help was 230352 Z, sent at 8 minutes before 1 P.M. Korean time on January 23.

This time difference between Wonsan, Honolulu, and Washington is important, because to get action on an urgent message is much easier at noon than it is at midnight. It may take a half hour or more just to locate the official who can act on an urgent message—or for underlings to decide to wake him up in the middle of the night.

The *Pueblo's* message sent at 1252 Monday, January 23 (Korean time) went on the air at 2252 Washington time—8 minutes to 11 P.M. Sunday the date *before* it was actually happening.

A word about codes and security is also in order here. A good communications system must be fast, reliable, and secure. It takes time to code and decode a message, so making it secure from eavesdroppers slows it down. Almost all important messages are coded, partly to keep the enemy from knowing what is in them, and partly to prevent him from leading us astray with phonies.

But there comes a time when speed is more important than security. This is true of a message where the enemy already knows the information that is in it. In such cases, anything that delays the message helps the enemy—not us. There is such a thing as making our communications so secure that we don't get the word ourselves in time for it to be of any use. This is a simple lesson that we apparently will never learn.

Before World War II, our Navy fliers had to use code for reporting the ships and formation of any enemy fleet. The enemy admiral already knew what ships he had and what formations he had them in. I speak from sad experience when I say that coding a message in the open cockpit planes we had at that time was difficult, took time, and could produce garbles that gave our own admiral false information. But we had to do it anyway!

At the Battle of San Bernardino Strait, delays in getting urgent messages from Admiral Kinkaid (Seventh Fleet) to Admiral Halsey (Third Fleet) brought on a critical situation in which the fate of the Philippine invasion hung in the balance for several hours. Vital messages were being delayed so long by coding and decoding that Kinkaid, in desperation, finally broke into plain English, with messages that gave the enemy vital information, but which had to get through or else.

Twenty-five years later, we still find urgent messages with information fully known to the enemy being delayed in transmission for "security reasons." The delays were only on the order of a half to three-quarters of an hour, but in the *Pueblo* case, every minute counted. From the time of the *Pueblo's* first SOS until she was boarded was about one hour and five minutes. From then until dark was three hours and a half. The nearest planes that could get to the scene needed at least an hour's flying time after they were briefed, armed, and launched. Speed was much more important than security, at this point. But time was lost setting up secure scrambler circuits to put through phone calls which might just as well have been put out on a loudspeaker circuit for all the good this info would do the enemy.

Maybe things happened too fast and we were too unready to save the ship no matter how fast the information moved. But delaying it even one minute for security reasons helped nobody but the enemy, who already knew a lot more about what was happening than we did.

Pueblo's link with the rest of the world was the naval communications station Kamiseya, Japan, located a few miles from Rear Admiral Johnson's HQ in Yokosuka. All messages from *Pueblo* went to that station and then were rerouted elsewhere as necessary. The Com Station had no authority to act on any of *Pueblo*'s messages. It simply relayed them to the many interested parties by phone, land wire, or radio. When directed by higher authority, it could quickly set up hot lines or special clear channels that would get urgent messages to the Com Stations of higher authorities—although not directly to the boss man himself.

The various Com Stations act more or less like the phone operators on long distance phone calls. The East Coast operator can get San Francisco operator very quickly, but on person-to-person calls, it often takes some time to get the right parties on the line.

Pueblo broke radio silence and called Kamiseya January 22 around 6 P.M. on a hand-keyed frequency that was a sort of party line used by many ships. Kamiseya then began trying to set up a secure high-speed teletype circuit for *Pueblo*. This circuit was finally working about 1100 next morning, January 23, and was kept open between *Pueblo* and Kamiseya until 1435, when the ship was boarded and captured. Radio operators kept up a continuous chatter on this circuit between official messages.

For the first two hours, the teletype traffic was pretty normal—two SITREPS, and a number of routine messages from the research unit reporting the technical data they had been gathering. SITREP 2 carried a "priority" precedence and was addressed to Rear Admiral Johnson for action and the following for information:

Commanding General, Fifth Air Force
Commander in Chief, Pacific
Commander in Chief, Pacific Air Force
Commander in Chief, Pacific Fleet

Chief of Naval Operations
Commander, Fleet Air Wing Six
Commander, Service Force Pacific Fleet
Commander, Seventh Fleet
Director, Naval Security Group
Fleet Air Reconnaissance Squadron One
HQ, National Security Agency, Pacific
Joint Chiefs of Staff
Naval Field Operations Intelligence Office
Navy Security Group Activity (Kamiseya)
Oceanographer of the Navy

It takes over five hundred characters to write all the above, but in the message heading it took only a four-letter group which had been set up ahead of time to mean all the above addresses. SITREP 2 came through just before noon, and *Pueblo* requested the circuit be held open for a while because "we have company outside."

An hour later, at 1252, OPREP 3/PINNACLE 1 came through reporting the signal, "Heave to, or I will fire." This was an official message (not radioman chatter) from the captain of the ship to Commander Task Force 96. Twenty-three minutes later at 1315, Bucher sent OPREP 3/PINNACLE 2. This was the last message classified by the Navy as "official" received from the CO of the *Pueblo*. For the next hour and twenty minutes, HQ, Japan found out what was happening through the unofficial chatter of the operators. From then on, Bucher was too busy to write and release official messages. But from 1252 on, Kamiseya relayed all the chatter to Johnson's HQ in Yokosuka, and after about 1315, the chatter went on up the chain of command to higher HQs. For this "chatter" in full, see Appendix D.

By Navy standards, only two official messages were sent from the *Pueblo* about the boarding incident, those of 1252 and 1315 (Korean time). All the rest were unofficial. But, of course, when the world begins coming apart, a skipper doesn't have time to write official dispatches. The chatter kept HQ well informed as to what was actually happening, and some of the "chatter" was obviously originated by Bucher himself.

The *Pueblo*'s Immediate Superior in Command (ISC) to whom all her messages were addressed for action was Commander Task Force 96, Rear Admiral Johnson. The term "task force" usually conjures up a picture of three or four aircraft carriers, a couple of cruisers, and a dozen or more destroyers. But in this case, Task Force ninety-six consisted of the U.S.S. *Pueblo*. Johnson was also Commander Naval Forces, Japan (CNFJ), made up of a number of shore stations and some small craft.

At noon on the twenty-third, Johnson was in Tokyo attending a conference. The first messages from *Pueblo*, SITREP's 1 and 2, reporting being sighted and shadowed, caused no concern in his headquarters. They got routine handling by the staff duty officer.

From noon till 1252, while things were heating up off Wonsan as shown by the radiomen's chatter, *Pueblo*'s traffic got no farther than the staff duty officer. At 1252 the PINNACLE 1 message (Heave to, or I will fire) came in and went immediately to the Chief of Staff (COS). But this message also said, "Intend to remain in the area if practicable," so the COS decided this was just normal harassment, such as the *Banner* had experienced.

About twenty-three minutes later, at 1315, PINNACLE 2 came in, saying the gooks had tried to board and *Pueblo* was departing the area. At this point, the COS began to realize that things were getting serious. At 1330 he decided they *were* serious and hit the panic button. He fired a "special procedure" message up the chain of command, put in a scrambler phone call for Fifth Air Force HQ, and started action to notify Admiral Johnson in Tokyo.

A "special procedure" message is the most urgent kind that can be sent and gets a clear channel over all other traffic right up to the National Naval Message Center in Washington. At 1345, the COS got through to Rear Admiral Johnson by phone. Since it was not a scrambler circuit, he used guarded language, but got the idea across that the *Pueblo* was in bad trouble. Johnson was soon on his way back by helicopter and arrived at his FHQ in Yokosuka at 1505 an hour and twenty minutes later. By that time, *Pueblo* was in enemy hands and on her way in to Wonsan.

The COS finally got through by scrambler phone to Fifth Air Force HQ about 1400 and urgently requested help for *Pueblo.* The normal way of making such a request would be Tokyo to CINCPAC in Honolulu, and CINCPAC back to Fifth Air Force in Japan. But by previous agreement, CNFJ was authorized to deal direct with Fifth Air Force and Seventh Fleet any time a snooper ship got in trouble. From then until *Pueblo* went off the air, Fifth Air Force HQ and Seventh Fleet were cut in on all traffic from *Pueblo,* including the chatter.

That covers what Commander Task Force 96 did that afternoon to help the *Pueblo.* It's just about all he could do. He had no forces actually under his command that he could send to her assistance. All he could do was to relay her SOS to others who *might* help.

One of those who might have helped was Commander of the Seventh Fleet. But for unexplained reasons Commander Naval Forces, Japan never actually asked Seventh Fleet to help. He did promptly forward all of *Pueblo*'s messages to Seventh Fleet and perhaps he assumed that when a Navy ship says she is being boarded and sends an SOS no further request for help is necessary.

The only bright page in the *Pueblo* disaster is, ironically, supplied by the Air Force. As soon as Lieutenant General McKee, Commanding General of the Fifth Air Force, got word *Pueblo* was in trouble, he took immediate action on his own hook to help her. Without asking a by-your-leave from anybody, he launched planes with shooting orders and flashed word up the chain of command so they could stop him if they didn't like it. Unfortunately, reasons beyond McKee's control made it impossible for his planes to reach *Pueblo* in time. Approaching darkness required him to call off the mission and land his planes in South Korea. But this wasn't his fault.

The Navy had made no request to him for protection of *Pueblo* on this mission, so he had no planes earmarked for the job. On two previous missions of the *Banner* for which protection had been requested, he kept planes standing by on the runway, and could have had them over the ship several hundred miles away in forty-five minutes. In the case of the *Pueblo*, planes would have been standing by in South Korea only fifty miles away, and could have been over the ship in half an hour, if they had been requested. Since none had been requested, the only planes he had in Korea were armed with atom bombs and were unsuitable for a rescue job anyway. He couldn't use planes from Japan because of treaty limitations. So he had to call on the 18th Tactical Fighter Wing in Okinawa, seven hundred miles away from Wonsan.

The 18th Fighter Wing's planes were all busy on other jobs. They had to be recalled, refueled, and rearmed before they could start to *Pueblo*'s aid. This was done as fast as possible, but by the time they got off, it was too late. McKee let them go on and land in South Korea just before sunset to await orders the next morning which never came. McKee launched

under the doctrine of "hot pursuit" and was willing to inter-
pret that doctrine very liberally on the afternoon of January
23. But action the next day came under the heading of "retaliation" and authority for it had to come from Washington.
Washington decided, "No."

The first word General McKee's HQ got of the *Pueblo's*
trouble was by scrambler phone from Rear Admiral Johnson's
Chief of Staff in Yokosuka. This call was put in about 1330,
but didn't get through till around 1400. At first there was some
confusion that it might be a drill message, but that was soon
cleared up. The word got to General McKee himself about
1415.

McKee issued orders to Okinawa, "You are to launch as soon
as possible, proceed to Osan, Korea, refuel, and proceed to
scene at Wonsan Harbor and strike in *Pueblo's* support at any
forces opposing her."

The first planes took off from Okinawa at 1611. This was
less than two hours after General McKee got the word, which
is mighty fast work for an unscheduled mission. At that time,
the gooks had been in possession of the ship for one hour and
forty-one minutes. At 1645, CINCPAC advised McKee that
he estimated *Pueblo* was now in Wonsan. (She wasn't—and
wouldn't be for another couple of hours.) But General Mc-
Kee let his planes go on and land in South Korea to await
further orders. The first P-105s got there at 1735, just six minutes before sunset and about half an hour before dark, by
which time *Pueblo* was nearing Wonsan Harbor.

So—although this effort accomplished nothing, it was a
very nice try. These planes had to be recalled from other missions, reserviced, and flown seven hundred miles from Okinawa to Korea. They got there just too late. If the Navy had
requested cover for *Pueblo's* mission ahead of time, those
planes would have been sitting on the runways in Korea, ready

to go, when *Pueblo* sent her SOS. They could have been over-head in half an hour and made a shambles of the four gook PT boats and two subchasers.

It may seem strange that in this day and age darkness should stop air operations. Airplanes can do many jobs at night now, but close support of ground forces is not one of them. For a job like helping the *Pueblo*, you've got to have daylight, or positive control from the ground at the scene of action.

The question naturally comes up, "Didn't the South Koreans have any aircraft we could call on for help?" General McKee thought of this, too, and queried the U. S. Army Commander in South Korea, General Bonsteele, about it as soon as the SOS came in. But when this question was raised a year later at a hearing by the House Armed Services Committee, the committee went into executive session to hear the answer. When the South Koreans asked us for help nineteen years ago, they got it fast and have been getting plenty ever since. So a public airing of the reasons why they couldn't help us might have made quite a bad smell.

My personal opinion is that we were afraid to turn the ROK Air Force loose for fear they would run amok and level Wonsan!

All this happened in the bailiwick of the Seventh Fleet, which is the striking force of the Pacific Fleet and a big piece of the whole Navy. It has three or four attack carriers, an antisub carrier group, the battleship *New Jersey*, and numerous cruisers, destroyers, and submarines. It also has a fleet of oilers, supply ships, and auxiliaries of all kinds that cut it loose from shore bases and enable it to stay at sea for months. The only other fleet like it in the world is the Sixth Fleet in the Mediterranean. We like to think that between the two of them, plus the First and Second fleets, which stay close to our own coasts, we have the ability to control the seas of the world.

Our only rival at sea is Russia, which has a fast-growing modern Navy that still lags far behind us. We pride ourselves on the overwhelming force that we can focus quickly on any point in the oceans of the world. These oceans cover 75 per cent of the earth's surface, and our fleets have planes and missiles that can reach two thousand miles inland, thus covering the entire surface of the globe.

However, there's a war on in Vietnam now, and we are so heavily committed there that it cramps our style elsewhere. Vietnam is two thousand miles from Korea, and it would take three or four days to redeploy ships up there.

But it so happened that on January 23, 1968, we had the *Enterprise* and several destroyers at sea about five hundred miles south of Korea. The *Enterprise* is one of our latest and biggest carriers, the only one with nuclear power. She can make 35 knots and carries an armada of our best jet fighters and nuclear bombers, for which five hundred miles is an easy hour's flight. She is the most powerful ship in the world, and in one deckload strike, she can deliver more explosive power than all the bombs dropped by both sides in World War II. On January 23 she had all her planes on board and no commitments for them.

An attack carrier at sea with her planes on deck is like the fire department. You don't have to call the fire house several hours in advance and notify them when your barn is going to burn. They are supposed to be ready whenever the alarm rings. So it is—or should be—on a ship like the *Enterprise*.

She can get into the wind and up to launching speed in five minutes. Even if all hands are in their bunks when general quarters sounds, she should be able to brief pilots and get the first planes off in one hour. Wonsan was five hundred miles away, another hour's flying time. If ordered to help the *Pueblo*, within two hours of the time she got the orders, she could have had a dozen fighters blasting the gook SCs and PT boats out of the water. If any of these planes ran short of gas for the return trip, U.S. air bases in South Korea were only fifty miles away.

The *Pueblo*'s troubles started about noon, and from that time until she was boarded and captured at 1430, she was in instant teletype communication with Navy HQ in Japan. At 1252, the gooks told her, "Heave to, or I will fire." At 1315 they opened fire on her. This news got to Japan as fast as it happened, and at 1330 Commander Naval Forces, Japan hit the panic button. This rang the fire alarm everywhere in the Pacific and in Washington, D.C. It was still four hours till sunset. *Enterprise* only needed two hours to get planes to the fire.

She never got them there. She didn't launch a plane. She reversed course and steamed north for a few hours at 20 knots and that is *all* she did to help *Pueblo*. In a good brisk wind, a full-rigged sailing ship could have done almost as much. If the Pentagon whiz kids ever set that problem up on their cost effectiveness computers, I'm afraid the sailing ship will show up much better than the *Enterprise* does.

Our control of the seas was challenged that afternoon, not by the fairly formidable Russian Navy, but by a rabble of SCs and PT boats in a gook hooligan navy. Our instant and devastating retaliation to their flagrant act of piracy on the high seas was to put them on the report to the United Nations in New York, two days later!

I feel sure that by the time this book is published, there will be some half-assed "explanations" from the Defense Department as to why the *Enterprise* didn't send planes.

The real explanation is simple—nobody had the guts to do it without orders from Washington—and orders never came.

In the chain of command that afternoon, there were two four-star and one three-star and one two-star admirals. I should think at least one of them would have issued shooting orders to help the *Pueblo* on his own authority. If Washington disapproved, the worst that could happen to him would be retirement a few years early—on three-fourths' pay. But no one was willing to stick his neck out that day, everyone waited for orders to do it.

Contrast this with an incident sixteen years ago that involved an Annapolis classmate of mine, Vice Admiral W. G. Schindler. Schindler commanded a task group in the Seventh Fleet in 1953, when one of our fliers had to ditch near the shore and not far from Vladivostok.

The flier got off a "mayday," and radio bearings indicated he was probably inside the three-mile limit in Russian territorial waters.

Schindler was in that area with a cruiser and some destroyers when he picked up the mayday. He immediately headed for the spot and cracked off the following dispatch to Commander U. S. Naval Forces, Far East:

From: Com Cru Div 3
To   :   Com Nav FE
Info :   Com Seventh Fleet, CINCPACFleet—CTF 77

Request you relay via appropriate channels to Russian authorities that if warranted by situation I intend to take my ships as close to Russian territory as is necessary to recover the airmen from the crashed aircraft and that furthermore, in the event I do, I will brook no interference.

The last line of this dispatch almost sounds as if it were lifted from Winston Churchill!

The reply Schindler got was simply, "Negative." However, by the time this reply came to Schindler's attention he had gone in, picked up the lone survivor from the crashed plane, and was back out in international waters.

The difference between Schindler's reaction in 1953 and the U. S. Navy's lack of action in 1968 is stark evidence of what Mr. McNamara's civilian control of the military has done to our flag officers in the past sixteen years.

On board the *Enterprise* that day was Rear Admiral H. H. Epes, Commander Task Group 775. His boss was Vice Admiral W. F. Bringle, Commander Seventh Fleet, flying his flag in the *Kitty Hawk*, at sea off Vietnam. Bringle was in constant touch with what was happening to the *Pueblo* from 1330 on. He relayed this info to Epes as fast as it came in and directed *Enterprise* to "proceed north at best speed. But take no overt action unless further informed."

It so happened that Admiral Sharp, Commander in Chief, Pacific, was in Vietnam that day conferring with General Westmoreland. He flew out to the *Kitty Hawk* that afternoon, landing aboard at 1700 and getting his first news of the *Pueblo*—although his HQ in Honolulu had known all about it since 1330. So there was a lot of horsepower off Southeast Asia that afternoon in the *Enterprise* chain of command—nine stars. The only action that all this talent produced was that *Enterprise* steamed north for a few hours at 20 knots. Period.

The only way I can explain this is: the admirals were handcuffed by the Pentagon's command system and couldn't move without prior approval from Washington—which they never got. Admiral Sharp intimated this plainly in his testimony before the House Armed Services Committee, but said he could not discuss this angle any further in open hearing.

But handcuffed or not, there comes a time when admirals should act, just as Bucher should have overridden his orders to keep his guns covered. If the admirals had started some action which Big Brother did not think wise, in this era of instant world-wide communications, B.B. could have stopped them.

Nothing whatever happened in the Seventh Fleet that afternoon. Big Brother didn't tell the admirals to do anything. The admirals did nothing on their own hook (except tell the *Enterprise* to reverse course for a couple of hours).

This is the way our armed services operate in 1968–69.

The next step up in the chain of command is to Honolulu, where the headquarters of two four-star admirals were located. CINCPAC, Admiral Sharp, was in theory the operational boss of all Army, Navy, Air Force, and Marines in the Pacific, including those in Vietnam. The admiral himself was, as we have seen, in Vietnam that day. The other HQ was that of Admiral Hyland, CINCPACFleet, and commander of all naval forces under Admiral Sharp.

You might think that when a Navy ship is boarded and captured on the high seas by pirates, it would produce instant and forceful action from the HQs of two four-star admirals. CNFJ's panic button alarm hit the fan in Honolulu about 7:30 P.M. Honolulu time. It upset the whole evening for both staffs. Admirals, captains, lieutenants, and sailors manned their battle stations and sweat blood till the small hours of the morning taking action to protect the United States against foreign aggression. They did this by promptly forwarding all the radio traffic from the Sea of Japan to the Pentagon. That's all they did. And there's no use writing a lot of words trying to make anything more out of it. That was *it*.

Commander in Chief Pacific Fleet played a key role in another case in which the Navy's public image took a beating —the Arnheiter case. Lieutenant Commander Marcus Arnheiter was a destroyer skipper in the off-shore patrol off

4

Vietnam early in 1966, who was relieved of his command "for cause" under strange circumstances involving anonymous letters written by disgruntled subordinates and charges of mutiny against the dissidents preferred by Arnheiter.

Arnheiter is a gung ho type. He is strong medicine, and people who have served with him either swear by him as an outstanding officer or say he is a phony and hate his guts. There is never a dull moment when he is around, and several times he has ruffled the feathers of sleepy seniors and got his own tail feathers scorched a bit for it.

The Navy's version of his relief is that he did a lot of nonregulation things trying to gain the spotlight and advance his own personal interests. His version is that he took command of a sloppy, ragtime ship and antagonized his subordinates by trying to straighten her out and make a proper man-o'-war out of her. Which version is correct, I do not know. It depends on whose witnesses you believe. I got interested in the case because, regardless of whether he was a good skipper or a Captain Bligh, I objected to the way he was knifed in the back by disgruntled subordinates. I claim that the Navy's action in his case lowered the authority of all other commanding officers.

Anyway, after a kangaroo court type hearing—which the Navy's lawyers claim with straight faces was legal—Arnheiter was relieved of his command "for cause." This wrote finis to his naval career, and ordinarily, that would have closed the case.

But not with Arnheiter. He fought back—in fact, is still fighting a forlorn and hopeless battle. For a while, this battle got national publicity and Congressional notice which was quite embarrassing to the Navy.

Commander in Chief, Pacific Fleet (not Admiral Hyland at this time) had a lot to do with the case. A junior admiral in the chain of command disapproved of the relief for cause, and went to bat for Arnheiter, recommending that he be given a second chance with another command. CINCPAC-Fleet overruled his subordinate, approved the relief for cause, and disapproved giving Arnheiter another chance.

The ironic part of all this is that one of the irregularities charged against Arnheiter was that he had wangled a lot of rifles and ammunition not on his ship's allowance list, and drilled his crew in using them to repel boarders. This was cited as a publicity stunt, which obviously had no bearing on preparing his ship for war in Vietnam waters. This was in 1966, two years before the *Pueblo* affair.

I think even CINCPACFleet will admit now that if they had given Arnheiter his second chance as skipper of the *Pueblo*, the *Pueblo* would not have been surrendered without a fight!

Hyland's immediate boss was another four-star admiral, U. S. Sharp—Commander in Chief, Pacific. His HQ is in Hawaii, very close to Hyland's and should have been able to authorize Hyland to use the Seventh Fleet and to order the Air Force to render whatever assistance Seventh Fleet needed. I doubt that it could—without getting an O.K. from the Pentagon.

When you get up on the CINCPAC level, you can't properly blame Admiral Sharp for any one of the many failures down the line. However, the *Pueblo* case was a major disaster and national disgrace. It happened in his bailiwick and "on his watch."

Of course criticizing the high command now for its inaction that afternoon is obviously Monday morning quarterbacking. The top admirals in the Pacific all feel that the way the thing happened, there was little they could have done to help the ship. It's very easy now to say that the *Enterprise* was only five hundred miles away and that the Commander Naval Forces, Japan hit the panic button four hours before sunset. But, they point out, there were only two official messages from the *Pueblo* and neither indicated anything more than the "normal" harassment we had come to expect from the North Koreans. There was unofficial chatter between radio operators indicating a lot more, but nothing from the commanding officer U.S.S. *Pueblo*. It simply takes time to realize that something fantastically improbable is really happening.

They say it would have been irresponsible and trigger happy to take action that might start a war, on the basis of unofficial radio operators' chatter. They say that by the time it became apparent the *Pueblo* actually had been boarded, all indications were that it was too late to help her. We know now that she didn't dock in Wonsan until 8:30 P.M. but so far as anyone could tell from the radio chatter that afternoon, the party was all over by 2:30 or 3:00 P.M.

They also point out that the weather that afternoon was not ideal for an air strike to help *Pueblo*—overcast, six thousand feet, breezy, with snow squalls. Finally they ask—even if *Enterprise* has interpreted the operators' chatter correctly, had guessed what was happening soon enough, and had launched planes to help her—and they had been lucky enough to find her—what could they have done?

Without attempting to evade the fact that "it happened on their watch," this is the way that the officers who bore the heavy responsibility of the high command feel about it. Perhaps those of us who had no responsibility and who criticize them now might have acted the same way had we been in their shoes.

But by time-honored military standards, when something

good happens in his bailiwick, CINCPAC gets the credit for it. When something bad happens, he has to share the blame.

The next step up in the chain of command is to Washington. Word got to the Chief of Naval Operations, Admiral Tom Moorer, at five minutes to midnight Sunday, January 22, Washington time. This was twenty-five minutes after CNFJ hit the panic button in Yokosuka on the afternoon of Monday, January 23. This was half an hour before the ship was actually boarded.

What happened in Washington in high-level circles from there on, present deponent knoweth not. Nobody who was in on the White House brainstorming sessions that night is willing to talk about it now. The manner of reaching the global strategy decisions that were made then will have to come from the memoir writers later. I'll read their versions of it with interest, but skeptically.

Whatever went on in these war room meetings, nothing came of it but talk. The second day after the capture, Secretary of State Rusk said at a news conference, "My strong advice to the North Koreans is to cool it." He followed that up the next day with a shattering verbal blast saying, ". . . the seizure was intolerable. There can be no satisfactory result short of prompt—may I may immediate—release of the ship and crew." Rear Admiral Smith of the United Nations mixed armistic commission in Korea served formal notice on the gooks: "The United States reserves the right to demand compensation for the seizure of this vessel." (NOTE—the rattling noise that was heard in Arlington about this time was just a lot of old sailors turning over in their graves.) The next day, the United States referred this matter to the Security Council of the UN and so far as I know, the council is still trying to figure out how to handle it.

So here we have a stark example of Mr. McNamara's

command as well as control of the military at work. We could have either saved the *Pueblo* on the way into Wonsan or gone in and brought her out the next day. But because of restrictions placed on so-called "operational commanders" in the past ten years, the admirals were unwilling to do it without clearance from Big Brother. They never got it.

Various reasons are given for refusing to let them act: "It might have started another major war, and we've already got our hands full in Vietnam." This says that a guerrilla war in Vietnam has so taxed the military resources of the United States that we can't defend our vital interests elsewhere. Hard to believe! Besides, even if we had to go into Wonsan Harbor to get the *Pueblo*, it would have been a relatively small naval job involving minor forces. It would have been done in a day, and *Pueblo* would have been either destroyed or towed out, most probably the latter.

To think that the Russians would interfere in a thing of this kind is absurd. They would have kept out for the same reason that we did nothing when they invaded Hungary and Czechoslovakia—fear of an atomic war. How could the gooks escalate in a way that would have been any real threat to us?

Fear of escalation should have deterred *them* from making the capture in the first place. It is clear, now, they knew they were dealing with a paper tiger, and had no fear of escalation. A firm reaction from us would have come as a rude shock.

Admiral Sharp, in his testimony before the Armed Services Committee, said, "Once the *Pueblo* entered Wonsan Harbor, any major U.S. countermoves would then be of a retaliatory nature. I therefore viewed the situation from this point on as one involving major U.S. forces in a confrontation that could result in a second Korean War."

Come, come now, Admiral! This is like saying that if someone punches you in the nose you won't punch him back because it might start a fight. It sounds more like some bright-eyed young "expert" from a think factory talking than it does like a four-star admiral!

Another reason given for our appeasement policy is that any action on our part *might* have resulted in the murder of our men. This is possible. But reprisal would not have meant certain slaughter. The lives of our boys depended entirely on a cold-blooded appraisal by the gooks as to whether it was worth while to keep them alive or not.

While the *Pueblo*'s crew were imprisoned, we lost over ten thousand Americans killed in Vietnam. But in the *Pueblo* case, we refused to defend our rights because it might cost eighty-two lives. Apparently, the Pentagon's cost effectiveness computers are programmed differently, when they calculate that one of these operations is worth while and the other is not.

By our action in the *Pueblo* case, we told bandit nations that all they have to do to put us over a barrel is to capture some American hostages. If we were a nation of hippies and flower children, this might be understandable. But we have the most powerful military force in the world and spend most of our national income supporting it. What good is it if it can't even defend our Navy against piracy?

Some will say that letting the admirals *act* in a crisis like this violates the principle of civilian control of the military. It does no such thing. If the government disapproves of what the admiral has done, it can very easily rectify it. We just return the ship to the gooks, apologize, and fire the admiral who rescued her.

As things turned out, we did not rescue our ship, but made an abject apology to the gooks anyway, a year later!

So much for the capture phase of the story. The piracy of a U.S. man-o'-war without a shot being fired and without a move on our part to rescue our ship made great face throughout the Orient for the gooks, and enabled them to ridicule the United States as a paper tiger. The gooks set out to milk all the propaganda they could out of this. What they wanted next was confessions, and films of our men humbling themselves before the brave soldiers of the People's Democratic Army of North Korea.

The gooks are past masters of extorting "confessions" using all forms of mental and physical torture. They use mental torture first, backed up by the constant threat of extreme physical torture—which they will use whenever necessary. In the case of the *Pueblo*, the physical torture was not necessary. Our men were humiliated and degraded and subjected to threats and some physical abuse. But you can hardly describe it as torture—at least, not physical torture. By our standards, they were treated like animals; but nowhere near as brutally as the gooks treat their own people. In fact, the gooks can probably say that, by their standards, our men were well treated.

All this means is that they were not beaten badly enough to inflict permanent injury or to have lasting scars, and that they got enough rice to keep them alive. They were carefully beaten and abused just enough to fill them with horror at what might be coming later.

Naturally, they put the pressure on Bucher first. They wanted him to confess that he had intruded on Korean territorial waters. He had not intruded, and at first refused to confess.

It didn't take them long to break him. Within forty-eight hours of the capture, they broadcast by radio what they claimed was Bucher's voice "confessing" to spying inside the territorial waters of the People's Democratic Republic of North Korea.

This had been a grim two days for Bucher. He was subjected to a constant barrage of questions, threats, and physical abuse. When this didn't break him they made him kneel, put a gun to his head, and said, "This is your last chance—sign our papers or you die." Bucher defied them to kill him, and says he prayed that they would. They carried that threat up to the point of pulling the trigger on the gun and claiming that it had misfired. Then they gave up threatening his life and made him think the lives of his men depended on what he did.

They showed him a South Korean prisoner, one of their own people. This man was pinned to a wall and had been beaten to a bloody pulp. His jaw was broken and hanging open. One eye had been gouged out of its socket and was hanging by a shred of flesh on what had been his cheek. The mangled wreckage of a face was barely recognizable through the clotted blood. This pitiful remnant of humanity was still alive. Bucher says this obscene exhibit made him throw up and faint.

The gooks said, "Sign—or we will do this to you." Bucher still refused.

While he was still shaken by this ghastly experience, they finally broke him down. They said, "Now we will bring your men in one by one, starting with the youngest, nail them to the wall and beat them to death right in front of you the way you have just seen—unless you sign."

This was too much for Bucher. He believed them, signed their false confession to save his men, while they made a film and tape of the signing.

After that, getting the crew to "confess" was fairly easy. There wasn't much point in the crew resisting after they had seen the movie and heard the tape of their captain's "confession." The gooks were thus able to get a group of about ten men to sign confessions and make a TV appearance agreeing to the confessions.

On this appearance, the famous obscene gesture bit occurred. Several men in the front row held their fists closed with the middle finger extended while the cameras were on them. Not being civilized, the gooks didn't realize what an impolite gesture this is. It cost Ted Williams a five thousand-dollar fine some years ago when he made it to the baseball fans in Boston—who, of course, are not civilized either. The gesture was spotted immediately when the pictures appeared in the United States, and the press made gleeful comments on it.

The savage reaction of the gooks to this gesture shows how far apart our two worlds are and how futile it is for us to try to understand them. They were not the least bit bothered by the fact that the gesture cast doubt on the truth—or willingness of the confession. It infuriated them because it made them lose face for having been outsmarted. It produced more beatings and physical abuse for our men—but only a reasonable amount, because they didn't want to kill any of them. The only reason they didn't was because as long as these men were still alive, they had bargaining value. This is the only value the gooks place on human life—"What can we get for it?"

I have no quarrel with Bucher or his men for signing the "confessions," nor with their conduct while prisoners. True, they violated Article V of the Code of Conduct prescribed for our service men by executive order of the President—which is a court-martial offense. But to court-martial these men would be so obviously outrageous that the lawyers have had to come up with some prize legal gobbledegook "explaining" why the executive order was not really binding and didn't apply to them. All of their reasons ignore the big reason— namely, that code is unrealistic and unworkable when we are dealing with barbarians. They also say nothing of the fact that the United States itself violated the code when we signed the official United States confession that got the boys released.

The present Code of Conduct is a product of the Korean War in the early 1950s. This war was our first encounter on a large scale with Communist torture of prisoners and the so-called tactic of brainwashing. Subjected to inhuman treatment by godless savages, many of our men cracked and made propaganda statements for the enemy—just as the *Pueblo* boys did seventeen years later. This was our first real experience with Communists—outside of the long-haired radicals in the United States—and caused great indignation among our people.

In 1955, I wrote an article for *The Saturday Evening Post* about brainwashing (see Appendix A) and proposed a way of

defeating it. My proposal was that the U. S. Government announce to the world through the United Nations that because
of the Reds' torture tactics and disregard of the rules of
civilized war, our men, when captured, would be allowed
from now on to appear on radio or TV programs, say anything
the enemy wanted them to say, and to sign any "confessions"
the enemy wanted. The purpose of this was twofold: (1) to
cut the ground out from under the propaganda value of such
"confessions" and (2) to save our men from pointless torture.

I was still on active duty at this time, and my piece in
the *Post* caused quite a flap around the Pentagon. Partly on
account of this piece, President Eisenhower appointed a
high-level commission to look into all aspects of this brainwashing business and to recommend what we should do about
it. I was a witness before this commission—and obviously, a
poor one. They finally came out with the present Code of
Conduct for Military Men, which reaffirms the Geneva Convention formula of name, rank, and serial number.

This formula is a relic of the days when wars were fought
by knights in shining armor. It comes down to us from the
times when wars were a game played by professional armies
on battlefields remote from large cities. The rules that they
made up for the game worked fairly well as long as it was
played only by the professional soldiers of "civilized" nations.
But times have changed. The entire population of civilized
countries participates in modern war, and a whole population
is nowhere near as disciplined and merciful as an army. The
target of a war is no longer the opposing army. It's the entire population of the enemy country—witness the arrays of
atomic missiles that the two leading countries of the West
keep zeroed in on each other's big cities. And even more than
that, wars are no longer fought only by enlightened civilized
nations. Barbarians like the North Koreans and Viet Cong are

getting into the act now. So the old rules of war are as obsolete now as bows and arrows and battle axes. But under the Code of Conduct, we still try to make our men live up to them—even though, as a matter of national policy, the country is committed to massive retaliation and genocide in the next big civilized war!

The crew of the *Pueblo* all knew in a vague sort of way about the Code of Conduct. All Navy men are instructed in it when they are recruits in boot camp. When the *Pueblo* was being taken into Wonsan, just before the first gooks got aboard, Commander Bucher got on the loud-speaker system and reminded all hands of the name, rank, and serial number bit. But they had gotten no special briefing on what sort of treatment they could expect if captured, and no instruction whatever on how to stand up under pressure when interrogated. Why should they? *Nobody* anywhere in the whole chain of command had even the remotest idea that these men might ever be captured.

You can't expect young Americans to stand up under Communist brainwashing and torture unless they have been well briefed and trained on how to resist it. Even then, I'm not sure all can hold out. But without training, they are clay pigeons for the Reds.

We attempt to train some of our fliers and the Green Berets in resistance. It is a rough program, and whenever an enterprising reporter writes a piece about it, howls of anguish go up from the longhairs and sob sisters about brutality.

But brainwashing is a brutal art, and you can't teach men to fight it by reading Emily Post to them. You've got to give them samples and let them see how sour it tastes. This is much better than getting their first taste of it in captivity. To throw a group of eighty-three completely untrained young men to the wolves as we did with the *Pueblo* is inexcusable.

Here was a group of young men who had grown up in a permissive society where the flouting of authority was an everyday fact of life. They were accustomed to confrontations between authorities and law breakers in which the authorities were handcuffed by rules designed to prevent police brutality. They had seen gangsters on TV contemptuously defy the U. S. Senate by taking the Fifth Amendment and refusing to answer. In all their experience at home, a prisoner's rights were zealously protected.

Now they were about to be captured by barbarians, whose normal method of operation was savage brutality. The Fifth Amendment, which stops probing senators in their tracks, would be no good against Communist tortures.

Our men were totally unprepared for what they were about to face. But they shouldn't have been. It was exactly the same brand of savagery that our men had been subjected to by these same North Koreans seventeen years before.

These gooks regard prisoners as cattle, to be used in whatever way best serves the owner's purpose, as they would use cows or pigs. Of course, most cattle owners show some regard for the comfort and well-being of their animals—but not the North Koreans. However, just as animals differ in value, so do prisoners; and the gooks treat them accordingly. Live Americans are of some bargaining value, so they try not to kill them. Prisoners who are the gooks' own countrymen are of no value, so they use them as horrible examples to extort what they want from Americans.

It's hard to see what we gain by requiring our men to submit to torture before they confess. The experts and the books written by those who have been through the mill agree that one big reason for holding out is the effect which it has on the man himself. If you hold out, you can look yourself in the eye forever after. If you don't—you lose some of your self-respect, which you never regain. So they say.

I cannot see why this should be true. But if it is, it is because a prisoner who confesses feels guilty about it. This can only be because he feels that he has betrayed his country and has not lived up to what was expected of him.

I feel that adopting my proposal would eliminate any guilt feeling. Our men would know that we would not hold them responsible for anything extorted out of them by torture or the threat of it.

The experts claim that this still wouldn't protect our men from being tortured. They say that if you confess, the Reds have nothing but contempt for you and will treat you even worse than if you hold out.

This simply underlines the vital importance of Item #2 in in the present Code of Conduct—"I will never surrender of my own free will." We must impress on our men that the Geneva Convention means nothing to savages, and anyone who is captured by the Reds is in for a grim experience. There is only one sure way to prevent godless savages from torturing helpless prisoners just for the sadistic pleasure of humiliating their betters. That is—don't get captured.

I feel the least we can do for those unfortunates who do get captured is to let them know we will not hold it against them if they crack.

It is worth noting that the only thing these strange people wanted from Bucher and his men was propaganda—confessions. They were not interested in any military or technical information. Perhaps one reason was that since they had the whole ship and all its papers and equipment, there was no need to seek technical information. Another plausible reason is that they were too stupid to realize what a haul they had made, and it wasn't of much value to them anyway, so they just turned it all over to the Chinese. This just confirmed all our previous experience with them in the Korean War, in which the main thing they wanted out of prisoners was propaganda—not military information.

Our national philosophy of life, our morality and system of values is so different from theirs that it is difficult for us to understand their motives. To us, an extorted confession is of no value, and makes those who produce it look evil and stupid. But in the Orient, a confession is a confession, and it's an important document no matter how you get it. The one who confesses loses face. Whether the confession is true or not makes little difference.

The fact that we disavowed their confessions, that they had obviously been obtained by torture and were not true, didn't matter to them. This peculiar attitude was highlighted in the negotiations to obtain release of the *Pueblo's* crew. The official representative of the United States, just before signing their papers admitting the *Pueblo* had intruded on their territorial waters, made a public statement saying, "This stuff is a pack of lies." This made no difference whatever to the Koreans. But the impolite gestures that got into their pictures made a lot of difference. It made them lose face because they had been outsmarted.

This is the sort of thing we must bear in mind when we deal with this kind of people and when we frame a code of conduct for our men to follow. When we take prisoners, our intelligence experts are interested in technical or tactical information, which can help us in a military way. All theirs are interested in is propaganda.

When we prescribe a code of conduct for our men that is based on the assumption they will be captured by civilized human beings, we are playing into the hands of these savages. Such a code might be all right for a war against the British.

But it is of no use against a gang of godless gooks. It is like saying you've got to fight by Marquis of Queensbury rules in a barroom brawl—or telling the police they've got to deal with the Mafia as if they were law-abiding citizens. When, the Supreme Court *does* tell them this, the Mafia defies the cops just as the gooks defied the United States.

If we adopted the proposal I made fifteen years ago, we would, in effect, be making the impolite gesture the *Pueblo* boys did, but doing it on an international level. It would be effective for the same reason that the *Pueblo* crew's gesture was effective. It would outsmart the gooks and make them lose face. Just the public denunciation of their torture tactics to the rest of the world would make it worth while. And if they produced "confessions" after we had officially denounced them, they would look ridiculous.

The present code has had a fair trial now, and it hasn't worked. Of course, the untrained *Pueblo* crew were a bunch of lambs thrown to the wolves, but I feel that even if they had been well trained, "confessions" could have been tortured out of them. I believe that skilled and patient torturers can get a confession out of almost anybody, especially when they can use drugs, polygraphs, and hypnosis in addition to torture.

I say "almost" because there are some rugged characters who will die before they will give an inch, no matter what you do to them. My hat is off to such men. Any man who holds out against torture and survives should be given the Congressional Medal of Honor. This medal is awarded for action "above and beyond the call of duty," and I feel that holding out against torture qualifies as such action. Not many can do it, so we wouldn't be cheapening the medal.

As things stand now, we have a code of conduct based on a Spartan standard that perhaps only one man in a hundred can live up to. This is a little bit like saying that since some men can run a mile in four minutes, we will make that the standard for all healthy young men.

By changing the code we can gain a great deal by saving most of our boys from torture. It seems to me that this is a proposition on which we have much to gain and nothing to lose. If savages want a confession badly enough, they will be able to break a certain number of our men and get it, even though some rugged characters may hold out. So a Spartan code does not really help the country. It subjects those who finally break to senseless torture, and it makes the resistance of the real strong characters futile.

Let me make it quite clear that what I'm talking about is propaganda only. I certainly do not favor letting prisoners tell the enemy anything that will be of military value to him. I don't think such information can be extorted anyway. I do not favor letting prisoners squeal on their fellow prisoners to buy favors for themselves. Anyone who would do that certainly won't be deterred by any code of conduct. And finally, I must admit that no matter what we do, we can't guarantee that our men will not be tortured by a sadistic enemy just for the sheer pleasure of inflicting torture on their betters.

Actually, I wouldn't change the present Code of Conduct much from what it is now. I would delete just one sentence from it, the second one in Article V. This reads, "I will make no oral or written statements disloyal to my country and its allies, or harmful to their cause." At the same time, I would have the United States issue a proclamation to the world, through the United Nations, explaining what we were doing and why.

This statement should say that our own treatment of prisoners will be governed by the Geneva Convention whether they are from civilized or Communist countries. It should then document the whole history of brainwashing from the Moscow purge trials and Mindszenty case through the experiences of our POWs in the Korean War, and now the *Pueblo* case. It should state that our way of life, ideas of morality, and civilized behavior are so different from the Communists' that we cannot deal with them as if they were ordinary human beings.

We should go on to say that when our men are captured by civilized people we will expect them to conduct themselves in accordance with the Geneva Convention. But if captured by Communists, we do not prescribe rules for their behavior, because the tortures to which they will be subjected are inhuman.

For this reason, we would notify the world that any so-called "confessions" extorted from our men while prisoners of the Communists were meaningless.

There is another side to this coin that deserves careful examination. That is the fact that some of our men who have been through the mill as POWs favor keeping the code exactly as it is. I know several of them who were POWs during the Korean War, who were brainwashed and brutally tortured, and who didn't give an inch. They took the worst the gooks could dish out to them, which is inhumanly barbarous, gritted their teeth, and told their tormentors to go to hell. The ones I have talked to are quiet, unassuming lads, and when you first meet them you would never suspect they are made of any different stuff from the rest of us. But you soon find out they are.

I feel uncomfortable talking to these lads about changing the code because they have been put through the meat grinder, and I haven't—thank God. I doubt if I could stand up under the savage treatment that they did, and perhaps that's why I favor an easier code. But they wouldn't change a word in the present code. They say that if we give an inch on it, we will open the flood gates for many things that we can't tolerate.

They say it comes down to a matter of preserving your self-respect, and that if you go any further than name, rank, and serial number, the enemy loses respect for you and you lose it for yourself. One thing leads to another, and before long you give away information of value to that enemy and even betray your comrades in the camp to gain favors for yourself. This is difficult to believe, but these Spartan lads who have defied the torturers speak from bitter experience, and they say it's true. They have seen good men start off by giving a little bit under pressure and gradually crumble until they were ratting on their buddies.

I believe that POW groups are a cross section of our citizenry and are just about like the rest of the nation; that is, a small percentage are very strong characters with steel nerves and high standards who will resist torture to death without breaking. Another small percentage are worthless bums who will betray their country and their friends if there is something in it for them. The vast majority are patriotic Americans who will hold out as long as they can, but who can be broken by torture. I think a man's behavior in prison camp depends on the stuff he has in him and which of the above groups he belongs in. I don't think that what the Code of Conduct says makes much difference.

There is one particular POW of the Korean War whose story I must tell. He was a lieutenant when captured, was a POW for two and one half years, and is a Navy captain now. I will identify him only as Joe because, as will be seen, he did things as a POW which might be considered undignified now that he is a four-stripe Navy captain.

Joe is one of the iron-man breed who wouldn't go a word

beyond name, rank, and serial number. The Communists gave him a vicious working over for months trying to break him. They beat him, they tortured him, they threw him in solitary confinement for days at a time in a near-freezing hole in the ground.

He has some interesting ideas about torture. He says torture is a self-defeating business, because if you refuse to give in to it, nature comes to your rescue. You get numb, and it doesn't hurt so much any more. Joe criticizes the *Pueblo* crew for making things easy for their torturers by co-operating and helping them to inflict torture. They told of being forced to kneel across two-by-fours, which cut off circulation in their legs, and of holding chairs at arm's length until they collapsed. Joe says you should refuse to do such things. Make your captors do the things to hurt you—don't do it to yourself. He says they beat the hell out of him daily, but never could make him do anything that hurt himself.

So Joe was beaten, starved, and frozen for many months. This treatment and the rotten food they gave him upset his digestive tract and he began generating great quantities of gas in his intestines. Since there was nothing else to do, Joe occupied his spare time between beatings learning how to control the release of gas from his bowels. He got to be quite expert at it. He could ease it out gently a little at a time or he could save it up and let it go in one loud raucous blast.

After he mastered this art, he quit talking to his interrogators. When they asked him a question he would look them straight in the eye and rip out a sonorous, contemptuous fart. This infuriated the gook interrogators. It caused them to lose face with the guards and junior officers who were present when it happened. After three or four sessions—with vicious beatings in between—they finally gave up on him and let him alone thereafter.

So there you have one way of defeating the brainwashers. I doubt, however, that we could write that into a code of conduct. And I'm sure that most of us have neither the intestinal fortitude nor virtuosity to resist torture as Joe did.

When I try to pin down Joe and others like him as to what they accomplished by their heroism, they give answers that many of us in this cynical modern world find hard to understand. They say, "The main thing is the effect which it has on *you*. As long as you resist, you keep your integrity and self-respect. When you give in, you die internally. When the gooks find out they can't break you, even *they* respect you. If you crack, they despise you, and are apt to beat you all the more to show it."

I put what I thought was a rather brutal question to him and asked, "Do you really think this world is a better place to live in today because you resisted torture seventeen years ago?"

His answer told the story in four words, better than I could do it in four volumes. He said: "For ME, it is."

I tried to draw a line between agreeing to their propaganda and giving the enemy valuable military information—or squealing on your fellow prisoners. Joe wouldn't have any part of it. He says it's an all-or-nothing deal.

Although I have the greatest respect for Joe's opinion and those of others like him who didn't crack, I think they are too hard-nosed about this. I feel we should tell our boys to say anything the enemy wants them to for propaganda purposes, and *we should publicly notify the whole world we have done this.* I think this would cut the ground out from under them so far as their propaganda is concerned. Perhaps the absurd confessions they extort are useful to the Reds behind the iron curtain. They wouldn't go to such lengths to get them unless they were. But they are filling their people up with lies about us all the time anyway. So what difference does one or two more make? Nations whose opinion we value on this side of the iron curtain would pay no attention to such confessions. The Reds would make themselves look ridiculous if they used them.

Giving military information to the enemy is a different matter from propaganda. There are many angles to this, and perhaps the different services should have different rules. A foot soldier or marine, right after he is captured, *may* have knowledge of tactical matters, the deployment of units next to his, location of strong points, etc., etc., which might be of value to the enemy immediately after he is captured. Maybe an air crewman might have some too, though I doubt it. I don't think the average Navy prisoner—officer or man—has any because naval deployments change too fast. I commanded an Antisub Killer Group in World War II, and if I had been captured, I don't think I could have told the Germans anything that would have helped them to win the war. I had no knowledge of high-level strategic plans—no information on D-day—knew nothing of the atomic bomb. Anyone who does have this kind of vital strategic information should never be allowed to get into a spot where he might be captured.

A glaring violation of this rule occurred in Korea, when General Dean was captured. Dean was the top U.S. commander in Korea at the time. He was captured wandering around in the front lines trying to rally his disintegrating troops when they had us on the run early in that war. The only way I can explain the gooks' lack of interest in brainwashing him is that they were sweeping everything before them at this time and it looked like they would soon run us into the sea. They probably didn't care much then what our strategic plans were.

General Dean got a hero's welcome when he finally got

back to this country. He also got a Congressional Medal of Honor, and not long after that we adopted the present code, which says, "I will never surrender."

POWs often have technical knowledge that would be of value to the enemy, and I certainly am not in favor of letting them spill it. But I don't think such information can be extracted from a man by torture unless he is willing to give it. I don't see how interrogators can know a plausible lie from the truth unless they know the right answer to begin with. If they do—what's the use of asking questions?

I knew some things about ASW (Antisubmarine Warfare) tactics and weapons which might have been useful to the Germans if I had ratted and told them. But I also think I could have told them some plausible fairy tales that wouldn't have done them a damn bit of good. If they had tortured me I don't see how they could have known when I quit telling fairy tales and started telling the truth—unless they already knew the truth.

Our intelligence experts tell me I'm all wet on this. They modestly claim that all intelligence experts are very shrewd operators. They say a skilled interrogator will easily sift out true from false and get plenty of pay dirt if you give him anything more than name, rank, and serial number.

But intelligence experts have told me lots of other stuff that didn't turn out to be exactly so. I'm a little reluctant to swallow this bit.

The *Pueblo* affair is a disgraceful humiliation unequaled in our history or in the history of any other great nation. It is much too big a blot on the national honor to call for scapegoats. There is shame enough in it for all, and the only shoulders broad enough to take the blame are those of Uncle Sam himself.

Grievous mistakes were made, but there should be no thought of punishing anybody. None of the wrongs were committed for personal gain or lack of patriotism. They were all simply blunders, caused by honest stupidity in high places and lack of guts.

But we can't just sweep the whole thing under the rug and forget it. The blunders cry to heaven for exposure in the hope that perhaps they will not be repeated again too soon. What follows is a list of some of the major ones.

The *Pueblo* was a makeshift right from the beginning, a product of Mr. McNamara's cost effectiveness program. She was hauled out of moth balls and converted from a cheap little tramp steamer to a floating electronics laboratory jammed full of black boxes that cost more than the whole ship did originally. It was the best equipment that our scientific know-how could produce for probing the "adversary's" electronic secrets. Apart from the actual cost of the black boxes, the research and development that went into them was priceless. But in the name of cost effectiveness, we put all these golden eggs into a cheap paper bag.

When the whiz kids set this up on their computers, I'm sure it came out as being cheaper and much more cost effective than building a proper new ship from scratch. But there are many factors affecting a problem like this that can't be set into a computer, such as the workings of the Oriental mind and the value of our national prestige and the value of the eighty-three lives of her crew. When you leave those out, the *Pueblo* conversion makes sense. The whiz kids can add it to the long list of items on which they claim to have "saved" the taxpayers billions of dollars—such as the TFX and aircraft carriers without nuclear power. This just verifies what computer experts call the "GIGO" factor (Garbage in—garbage out).

The blame for this mistake can be split two ways. Half goes to the whiz kids and their computers. The other half goes to the Navy for tolerating them.

The next blunder was in refitting the ship, when no provision was made for scuttling or instant destruction of the black boxes. Blame for this goes to the Navy. Bucher wrote letters about this, requesting proper equipment, but they were pigeonholed. The excuse now is "lack of funds." This is always a ready alibi for bureaucrats. The only way you can dispute them is to point out that the amount involved is an absurdly tiny fraction of the Navy's annual appropriation of billions.

The basic planning for this operation was utterly naïve. It

was done by professional military men all the way up the chain of command from Rear Admiral Johnson in Japan to the Joint Chiefs of Staff. Johnson's staff in Yokosuka were right at the scene of action and should have been the experts on local conditions. In Honolulu the large staffs of two four-star admirals pondered over it. In Washington the JCS, presumably the best military brains in the country, studied it. The whole intelligence community, CIA, DIA, NSA, and ONI (Office of Naval Intelligence) were all available to advise. The verdict was the same all the way up the line: "minimal risk—unnecessary to make any provision for defending the ship."

After what happened to the *Pueblo*, this seems incredible. Of course, those who made the mistake can say, "any dumb cluck can see the danger now, but it's hard to foresee piracy on the high seas when it hasn't happened in 150 years." This is quite true; although in this case, we had specific warning ahead of time from the Korean radio, which the "experts" didn't believe. And no matter how tolerant we are inclined to be toward the individuals who guessed wrong, this is a glaring indictment of the military planning system. This is the system on which the fate of the nation may someday depend.

Another flaw in the planning system exposed by this fiasco is the futility of our so-called "contingency plans." All military commands have detailed plans prepared ahead of time for every situation which they can foresee. Then, if situation X comes up, a simple message from HQ, "execute plan X," tells everyone exactly what he is to do. We even have plans for unforeseen situations known also as "contingency plans." These set up chains of command, communication circuits, and task groups without specifying exactly what they are to do. Then if an emergency comes up, not covered by other plans, a

dispatch "execute contingency plan" will at least get everybody alerted for the detailed instructions that will follow
later.

The *Pueblo* case showed that in a fast-breaking situation,
these plans aren't worth the paper they are written on. The
fatal flaw is that no one in the fleet has authority to execute
them. Four-star admirals can move ships around on routine
peacetime missions, can run fleet exercises, and can approve
bales of paper plans drawn up by their staffs. But when one
of our ships is wantonly attacked on the high seas, they can't
do a damn thing about it. They've got to get on the scrambler
phone to the Pentagon and say, "Oh, sir! What shall I do?"

In the *Pueblo* case, by the time they got the answer, it was
too late to stop the seizure, and Washington didn't have the
guts to authorize recovering the ship.

Another glaring mistake in preparing for this mission was
Rear Admiral Johnson's order to Bucher to keep his gun
covers on. If the very sight of these guns was enough to
antagonize an adversary, or if the guns were so puny they
could be of no use, they never should have been put aboard
in the first place. But once they were on board, telling the
skipper to keep them covered is stup— er . . . ill advised.
This is the sort of an order that should be disobeyed when
the time comes. But Bucher obeyed it, literally.

This brings us up to the actual surrender off Wonsan.

Bucher decided to surrender without firing a shot, in order
to save the lives of his men.

This decision was wrong. He should have fought as long as
he was able to fight. This is what the naval regulations and
long-standing naval tradition require.

A merciful government—embarrassed by its own failures
has now pardoned the human weakness that caused sur-

render. But to approve it as a standard for the future is unthinkable.

The faults chargeable to Bucher are:

(1) Surrender without a fight.

(2) Failure to disobey an ill-advised order.

(3) Making no attempt to scuttle or disable his ship.

To try to make anything heroic out of Bucher's conduct is absurd. But a congressman from Nebraska has actually introduced a bill to give him the Congressional Medal of Honor! I trust Bucher would have the common sense to decline this decoration in the improbable event that the bill should pass.

Bucher got the Purple Heart medal—awarded for "wounds inflicted by the enemy." That's all he deserves.

The Navy should now let him serve out his time for retirement in jobs where he will not be called upon to make any big decisions.

Now we come to the high echelon faults in the Navy chain of command that afternoon. They were many, and extend clear up to the top. *Pueblo* sent out her SOS four hours before sunset, and seven hours before she was finally tied up to the dock in Wonsan. The United States has airfields in South Korea, Japan, and Okinawa, and the U.S.S. *Enterprise* was only five hundred miles away from Wonsan. No help whatever was given to the *Pueblo* that afternoon. She might as well have been in the Sea of Tranquillity on the moon, instead of just across the Sea of Japan.

That afternoon there were four admirals in the Pacific who could have given the *Enterprise* orders to launch planes in response to the *Pueblo's* SOS. They were a rear admiral in the *Enterprise,* a vice admiral in command of the Seventh Fleet, and two four-star admirals in Honolulu, CINCPAC-Fleet, and CINCPAC.

The only command that even tried to help the *Pueblo*
was the Fifth Air Force, using planes based on Okinawa.
General McKee had not been requested to cover the *Pueblo*
so his planes were all busy on other jobs. But as soon as
he got *Pueblo*'s SOS he recalled his planes, armed and refueled them, briefed the pilots, and launched planes with
shooting orders. The first planes got off one hour and twenty-
three minutes after McKee issued his orders. Wonsan is seven
hundred miles from Okinawa and the planes couldn't quite
get there before dark. They landed to refuel in South Korea
just before sunset and were held on the ground there. But
they had made a nice try.

The *Enterprise* had all her planes on board, no operations
scheduled, and she was only five hundred miles from Wonsan.
The only action taken on the *Enterprise* when *Pueblo*'s SOS
came in was to break out the reference books and try to find
out what kind of a ship *Pueblo* was!

Commander Seventh Fleet's only other action on the SOS
was to direct *Enterprise* to steam toward Wonsan at best speed.
It took forty-six minutes for this urgent operational message to
reach the *Enterprise*. But this didn't really matter much because the message also said, "Take no overt action until
further informed."

This is incomprehensible.

At the Congressional hearings on the *Pueblo*, the CNO
and the CINCPAC Pacific tried to defend this inaction. So did
General Wheeler, Chairman of the JCS. What else could they
do? When the blame for a series of blunders extends all the
way up the chain of command you can hardly expect anyone
in the chain to put the finger on a subordinate. All these
distinguished officers spoke in Pentagon gobbledegook about
the "time distance frame" making it impracticable to help
Pueblo that afternoon.

This was a lot of hogwash.

The following table shows the "time distance frame."

DISTANCE *Enterprise* TO WONSAN—FIVE HUNDRED MILES

Time (*Korean*)

1252   *Pueblo* sends PINNACLE 1 ("Heave to, or I will fire")

1315   *Pueblo* sends PINNACLE 2 ("Attempting to board")

1330   *Pueblo* sends SOS. Koreans open fire

1330   Commander Naval Forces, Japan hits panic button sounding alarm over entire chain of command

1430   Rear Admiral Epes in *Enterprise* and Commander Seventh Fleet get *Pueblo*'s SOS (one hour delayed!)

1432   *Pueblo* boarded by eight to ten gooks

1530   *Pueblo* at twelve-mile limit

1645   *Pueblo* at three-mile limit

1734   Sunset

1800   Darkness

2030   *Pueblo* alongside dock in Wonsan

The time from PINNACLE 1 to sunset was four hours forty-two minutes; from SOS to sunset four hours and four minutes, and from the time Seventh Fleet and *Enterprise* finally got the word until sunset was three hours and four minutes. The distance was five hundred miles.

It is simply absurd to say that the *Enterprise* can't strike a target five hundred miles away within three hours. The flight time is less than an hour. Any carrier at sea with all her planes on board should be able to launch a good-sized strike within an hour of getting a FLASH order to do so. This includes time to fuel, arm, respot the deck, and brief pilots. Lieutenant General McKee got his first planes off in an hour and twenty minutes and he had to recall them from other missions. Even the Navy's experts who were trying to justify the *Enterprise*'s inaction, admitted it could be done in an hour and a half.

Accepting the hour and a half figure, the *Enterprise* could still have gotten planes over the *Pueblo* by 1700, thirty-four minutes before sunset and one hour before dark, when she was just inside the three-mile limit. These planes could have made a shambles of the Korean small craft that were molesting the *Pueblo*.

Whether the eighty-two surviving Americans could then have recovered the ship from the small Korean boarding party is another question. I think they could have. But we will never know.

All that stuff about "time distance frame" adds up to a rather shocking confession by the Navy, namely, that its reaction time to a grave emergency is something more than three hours! In this atomic age when the outcome of a big war can be decided in half an hour, this is not good enough. Unless our attack carriers can do better than that we might as well put them in the moth ball fleet.

One lesson to be drawn from this fiasco is that modern technology has outstripped our ability to use it. It has given us powerful weapons systems and instant world-wide communications. But the men in command are too slow in making up their minds and accepting responsiblity for important decisions.

In any sort of an organization, government or private, there are two ways in which a subordinate official can act when some unforeseen crisis comes up in his bailiwick:

(1) He can use his best judgment, decide what should be done and go ahead and act—keeping his bosses informed about what he is doing so they can stop him if they want to.

(2) He can just refer the problem up the line to higher authority and let them act.

Course #1 can involve some personal risk. If what the man does turns out badly, or even if his superiors think it may and stop him from doing it—it may cost him his job. Of course, if it turns out well, his superiors will say, "That's exactly what I would have told him to do if he had asked for instructions." He gets a nice pat on the back.

Course #2 involves the risk that nothing at all will be done. If the upper echelons of the organization work the same way as the low-level ones where the problem originated, the request for instructions simply gets bucked all the way up the line to the top man. By the time he decides and passes the word back down the line, it may be too late for the proposed action to do any good. But everyone in the chain of command has kept his finger on his number and nobody gets hurt, except maybe some small boy down at the bottom where the problem arose.

This may be all right in a business organization, where all you can lose by being wrong is money. But in a military organization it's intolerable. It produces *Pueblo* incidents. In an outfit where everyone is supposed to be ready to die for his country if necessary, the officer in charge should certainly be ready to risk his career for it when an emergency requires quick action. This is the way it used to be in the Navy that I served in for forty-three years.

But we've had twenty years of Unification and denigrating the brass now, and six years of Mr. McNamara and his whiz kids. More and more, initiative has been curbed on low levels and authority to act concentrated in the Pentagon. The top officers of all services now have spent half their careers in this atmosphere. They at least know how things *used* to be done. But we have a whole generation of officers just coming up for flag rank now who have spent their whole careers under the play-it-safe system, and who wouldn't be coming up for promotion unless they had conformed to it.

We can therefore expect more *Pueblo* cases from now on.

The faults chargeable to the naval high command that day are:

(1)   Failure to plan any support for *Pueblo* ahead of time.

(2)   Failure to send help from the *Enterprise*.

(3)   Failure to ask South Koreans for help.

(4)   Failure to go in and get *Pueblo* the next day.

This carries the story up to the doorstep of the U. S. Government in Washington. This is where the major blame for the fiasco belongs. But trying to pin blame for specific mistakes on anyone in Washington is, of course, futile. The officials involved are the Chief of Naval Operations, the Joint Chiefs of Staff, the Secretary of Defense, Secretary of State, the National Security Council, and the President. When you get up on that level, responsibility for anything bad is a very elusive thing, and everyone can always blame someone else.

In the Bay of Pigs snafu, it was so complicated that even President Kennedy couldn't pin it down. But he was the Captain of our Ship of State, so he finally took thought of his Navy training, stepped forward, and said, "*I* was responsible."

In many ways, the *Pueblo* case resembles the Bay of Pigs. In both cases, trusting young men were sent on dangerous missions, confident that they had the full military might of the United States behind them. When the going got tough, we abandoned them. At the Bay of Pigs, we threw a lot of bright-eyed young Cubans to the wolves. But in the Bay of Tong Josan, it was our own sailors that we abandoned.

The blame for this belongs mostly to the Defense Department, but Mr. McNamara has made no move to accept it.

The big thing that the Defense Department did wrong in the *Pueblo* case was that it did nothing. This is the result of seven years of centralized control of everything from the Pentagon by the McNamara regime, which has stifled the initiative of responsible officers in the field. No crises of any importance can be resolved now except in the ivory tower of Sec Def's office. Even if all the decisions of this office were infallible, this system would be no good. In cases like the *Pueblo*, decisions cannot be made and gotten back to the people who have to execute them in time to be of any use. The *Pueblo* is a flagrant example of inability to act fast when commanders on the spot are handcuffed. Communication is simply not good enough.

This may seem strange in this era of almost instant communication with anywhere in the world by long-distance phone, radio, TV, and satellite relays. You can sit in your living room now and actually watch a soccer game in Australia while it is being played. The action on the tube of your TV is only microseconds behind that in the field. Apparently the Big Brains in the Department of Defense feel that they can be in touch with military events on the other side of the world the same way.

We have a special communication system for our Polaris subs that *does* work that way. But this system is designed to trigger the end of the world when and if the Big Brains decide that this is the logical thing to do. Quite properly, this must be an instantaneous system. But for smaller crises, such as piracy on the high seas, communication isn't that fast.

The radio waves travel just as fast. But the problem is getting them to penetrate the protective screens of aides and secretaries that surround the Big Brains who make the decisions. When Bucher marked his SOS "CRITIC," he thought he was putting it on a direct line to the White House.

Actually, it had a long, uphill haul getting there. Just how long it took is classified as secret by the Navy because "giving the exact time would reveal the capability of our communication system." I agree with that general idea, but would use a little different word and say, "*in*capability."

But failure to act the day after the capture cannot be excused by delays in communication or lack of time. Our government simply lacked the guts to go into Wonsan and recover the ship. One reason given is that this might have antagonized the gooks. Admiral Sharp said, "It might have resulted in another major Korean war."

So we simply "turned the other cheek." This may be good Christian ethics, but it doesn't apply when dealing with godless savages. If we adopt that as a national policy, we can expect to be humiliated by third-rate nations whenever it suits their purpose. Even the Gospel says, "When a strong man armed keeps his house, those things which he possesses are in peace."

The faults for which Washington is to blame in the *Pueblo* affair are:

(1) The system of command control, which handcuffs military commanders in the field and makes them come to Washington for authority to act, even when immediate action is urgent.

(2) Failure to order *Enterprise* to rescue *Pueblo* on the afternoon of January 23.

(3) Failure to order CINCPAC to enter Wonsan Harbor next day and bring *Pueblo* out.

Since public sympathy in this affair was clearly on the side of Commander Bucher, it is well to take a close look at some of the basic principles involved.

A Navy court of inquiry, consisting of five admirals, spent over a month looking into this thing, and did a good job, as far as it went, which was only up to the first level of command above the *Pueblo*. Of course, blunders were made clear up the chain of command all the way to the White House, so the court merely exposed the tip of the iceberg. But that's all this court was supposed to do.

You certainly can't expect a court of Navy admirals to point an accusing finger at anyone senior to them in the chain of command. Had it done so, it would have shown lack of common sense, raising grave doubt as the the fitness of its members for promotion to high command themselves.

The big question that this court had to answer was a very simple one—"When a U. S. Navy ship, engaged in its country's business, is confronted with superior force, should it surrender?"

The court's answer was, "No. The skipper who does surrender should be court-martialed." I fully approve of this verdict.

The Secretary of the Navy, exercising his civilian control, decided that because of the many high-level blunders that put Commander Bucher on the spot, there would be no court-martial. This was all right too.

The professional Navy had to take a hard-nosed view of this matter. If it had officially condoned surrender without a fight, it would be time for the Navy to go out of business and turn its job over to the Coast Guard.

At 0352 Z on January 23, 1968, Commander Bucher was on the horns of a grim dilemma. He had a perfect right to be where he was and doing what he was. Navy tradition and regulations said, "Fight, no matter what the odds." But Bucher was convinced that fighting would not save his ship and would result in the slaughter of his crew. He thought the only way to save his crew was to surrender. Surrender would violate three of the great guiding laws in a naval officer's code: (1) The Navy Regulations (2) Executive Order 10631 (Code of Conduct for the Military Forces), and (3) long-standing hallowed Navy traditions.

Article 0730, Navy Regulations, reads: "The commanding officer shall not permit his command to be searched by any person representing a foreign state nor permit any of the personnel under his command to be removed from the command by such persons so long as he has the power to resist." Navy regulations are federal law, so far as the Navy is concerned.

The Code of Conduct says:

"1. I am an American fighting man. I serve in the Forces which guard my country and our way of life. I am prepared to give my life in their defense.

"2. I will never surrender of my own free will. If in command I will never surrender my men while they still have the means to resist."

Naval tradition also says that U.S. men-o'-war do not surrender. They go down with guns blazing and colors nailed to the mast. Navy regulations cover practically every problem that can ever come up aboard ship—except how to surrender. Until the *Pueblo* case, all Navy men accepted it as one of the facts of life that you never surrender.

Commander Bucher chose to do so. The Navy is now officially on record condemning his action.

Bucher's defenders justify what he did by saying that to fight meant certain death for all hands and would serve no useful purpose. But we will never *know* what would have happened if he had chosen to fight. Perhaps he and his whole crew would have been slaughtered. But *maybe* the gooks would have put their tails between their legs and run. "Hopeless" causes have often been saved by putting up a fight against the odds. The *Pueblo* gave up without taking her gun covers off.

Besides, surrender to a gang of ruthless savages gave Bucher no assurance that the lives of his crew would be spared. In fact, later his captors threatened to beat his men to death one by one in front of him unless he signed a false confession. Bucher says under oath he believes they would have done it.

Suppose he had chosen to fight, and his crew had been slaughtered. Would their deaths have been useless? That depends on how you value certain things.

One of the big differences between our way of life and the Communists' is the value we place on human life. It has become popular these days to say that preserving human life takes precedence over everything else.

This sweeping generality just doesn't hold water. If we really meant that and intended to live by it, the Communists would soon rule the world, and we would have their low valuation of life rammed down our throats.

And obviously we don't believe our own valuation. Otherwise, how do you justify our fleet of Polaris submarines with their nuclear missiles constantly zeroed in on the big cities of Russia, aimed, cocked, and ready? If we ever turn these missiles loose, one hundred million human lives will be snuffed out. The countdown for this holocaust right now, at this very moment, is "one minute and *holding*."

How does this jibe with the idea that preservation of human life takes precedence over everything else? Obviously there are other things to which we give higher precedence—one of them being preservation of freedom. Perhaps honor, patriotism, and duty to God and country should have a higher place too.

If the *Pueblo* had fought, her men would not have died uselessly. The biggest thing the Koreans got out of the *Pueblo's* capture was a smashing propaganda victory. A ship of the supposedly invincible U. S. Navy was boarded and captured by the tiny navy of the Republic of North Korea. The Reds broadcast to the world, "Confronted by the brave sailors of the People's Democratic Republic, the cowardly imperialist warmongers surrendered without even a fight."

In the Orient, "face" is one of the most important facts of life. The United States can never regain the face it lost in the *Pueblo* fiasco. Propaganda is what the Koreans were after, and they reaped a bonanza of it. They also got a windfall of top-secret intelligence papers and our most hush-hush electronic black boxes. But this stuff was of no interest to them. They gave it all to the Chinese. What they wanted was to humble the United States and gain face for themselves in the Orient. This they did, beyond their wildest dreams.

If they had taken the *Pueblo* after a bloody fight, the propaganda value would have been small. But taking it as they did was the greatest Oriental victory over the West since Pearl Harbor. We will not live it down in our lifetime. Even among our friends and allies, we lost face.

This matter of face requires a word of explanation. Most Occidentals have no real idea of what it stands for in the Orient. They think it is more or less the same as status, dignity, a social standing. But these things are merely the trimmings of face. It means far more than that. It means honor, integrity, trustworthiness, and everything of moral value. When an Oriental loses face, he is utterly degraded and becomes a nobody. It's almost as bad as having all your credit cards revoked in our Great Society. And usually, you can only lose it once. Once you have lost it, a lifetime is too short to regain it.

This is what happened to the United States throughout the Orient when the *Pueblo* surrendered without a fight. We are powerful enough so that we are still feared. But we are no longer respected.

At Pearl Harbor, we were humiliated; but whether we lost face or not remained to be seen. It depended on what came after. What came after eventually turned the tables, and the Japanese were the ones who lost face. The Koreans expected a violent reaction to the capture of the *Pueblo*. It never came. A year later, to get the crew back, we meekly signed a "confession" that we had violated their territorial waters. We will never gain back the face we lost by this.

The last time a U. S. Navy ship was boarded on the high seas without a fight was in 1807. Then, H.M.S. *Leopard* boarded and searched the U.S.S. *Chesapeake* off our Atlantic

Coast and removed four of our sailors from her. This, and similar cases of shanghaiing our sailors off merchant ships, led to the War of 1812, fought primarily over the issue of freedom of the seas.

The captain of *Chesapeake* in 1807 was James Barron. He is remembered in history now as the man who killed Stephen Decatur in a duel over derogatory comments Decatur made about the boarding.

Later, the *Chesapeake* won herself a place in history. During the War of 1812, off Boston Harbor, she was boarded, captured, and taken to a British port by H.M.S. *Shannon*. Her captain, David Lawrence, and many of her crew were killed in this battle. Lawrence's dying words on his quarter-deck have become a watchword in the U. S. Navy. Ironically, they were, "Don't give up the ship."

Neither of these episodes in which the *Chesapeake* figured shed any glory on the U. S. Navy. But the second makes better reading in the history books than the first, even though no lives were lost when Barron submitted to search and seizure.

Incidentally, Article 0730 of Navy Regulations was written as a result of Barron's craven action.

Ever since "civilization" began, soldiers and sailors have been expected as a matter of course to be ready to die for their country. This has been one of the basic facts of life in the Christian era—and before. I know of no military man who has won an honored place in history by surrendering without a fight. Certainly Barron didn't! But we seem bent on giving Bucher one now.

This idea of valuing human life above all else is a high-sounding booby trap. It can lead to national suicide. If we really believe it, we can live in peace with the Communists and save a great many lives by simply doing what Bucher did—submitting. But, of course, what we will get for doing it will be the same as what Bucher and his men got during their year of imprisonment. Those who would "rather be Red than dead" can have their "druthers" any time they want them, at the price of slavery, as Hungary and Czechoslovakia are finding out.

We honor the early Christian martyrs now who chose death in the Colosseum rather than deny their faith. But *if* preservation of human life takes precedence over everything else, then these men and women were misguided zealots and fools!

The *reductio ad absurdum* of this preservation-of-life idea is the current wave of hijacking airliners. Airliner crews are supposed to be intrepid birdmen—adventurous, daredevil types. But whenever some greasy young punk pulls a knife on a stewardess . . . off we go to Havana. Nobody has the guts to find out that the hijacker really hasn't got any guts. This is just a miniature preview of how the Communists will take over the country someday if we keep on as we are going.

I had first-hand experience with this fallacy of preserving lives at all costs during my last tour of active duty when I was Commander, Caribbean sea frontier, in San Juan, Puerto Rico. We had an incident with Castro that turned out to be a miniature preview of the *Pueblo* affair.

In 1958 Castro was still a guerrilla; and he and his gang of bandits were hiding up in the hills of Oriente province at the east end of Cuba, near our naval base of Guantanamo. At that time, we allowed sailors from the base to make weekend liberties to nearby Guantanamo City. In the early hours of a Sunday morning, a bus bringing back thirty sailors to the naval base was hijacked by four of Castro's bandits and taken up to his hide-out in the hills about thirty miles from the naval base.

Our sailors were held captive for several weeks and newspapers friendly to Castro, like The New York *Times*, had themselves quite a story.

Guantanamo was part of my bailiwick, and these were my men. I wanted to send the Marines from the naval base up into the hills and rescue these men. But in these days of instant communication, you can't do a thing like that on your own. You must get an O.K. from the Pentagon. Admiral Arleigh Burke, the CNO at that time, was in favor of sending the Marines too. But when he, in turn, asked permission to do this the answer was, "No! The bandits might kill all our men." So the State Department, who were covertly backing Castro at this time, opened negotiations with him and about three weeks later, our men were returned. Meantime, Castro reaped a windfall of favorable publicity in our far-left press.

Incidentally, I met this group of sailors when they returned to the naval base and there wasn't a bullet wound, broken bone, or even a black eye among them. Talk about submissiveness! Here was a group of thirty American sailors who were captured and kidnaped by four crummy Cuban bandits. They came back without a mark on them.

This affair, disgraceful and humiliating as it was, was not as bad as the *Pueblo* affair. But our country's reaction to this flagrant crime against our sovereignty was exactly the same as in the *Pueblo* case. It was to get the boys back safely, no matter what the cost to our standing in the community of nations.

I wanted to get the men back—safely if possible—but to get them back as fast as the Marines could get to them. I am still convinced that Castro at that time was not crazy enough to murder our men. But if he had, you can depend on it, the Marines would have wiped out him and his whole gang. If this had happened, it would have changed the recent history of Latin America. There would have been no Bay of Pigs and no Cuban missile crisis, in which the world teetered on the brink of an atomic holocaust for several days. This world would be a better world to live in today, and our men would not have died in vain.

I wonder what those thirty men are doing now to make this a better world. I wonder if they will brag to their grandchildren that they were one of that submissive band who came back that morning without even a black eye?

By far the most important thing about this affair was the effect it had on Castro and on our standing in the eyes of all the other American countries. Here were thirty of our sailors, kidnaped in uniform, without even any pretense that they had done anything wrong. Our reaction was simply to say, "Tut, tut. You shouldn't have done that. Please, Mr. Castro, let us have our men back."

How could you expect Castro to have any respect whatever for this country after we let him get away with that? How could you expect other Latin American countries to respect us? Or Asiatic countries either, for that matter—where The New York *Times* circulates. If there were any lingering doubts after this happened about whether we were a paper tiger or not, the Bay of Pigs removed them.

The fatal error in this, as well as the *Pueblo* case, is the starry-eyed proposition that preservation of human life takes precedence over everything else in this world. This is one of those high-sounding ideas that we piously proclaim, but don't live by. Taking issue with it is like attacking home, mother, and the American flag. But to try to live by it is out of the question.

Automobiles kill over fifty thousand human beings in the United States *each year*. If we abolished automobiles, we could save all those lives. But obviously, getting where we

want to go in a hurry is more important than fifty thousand
lives. The fact that many of us, when we get where we are
going in such a hurry, will just sit down, scratch ourselves,
and have a drink, has no bearing on this subject.

In eight years of war in Vietnam, we have lost thirty-five
thousand men killed. We could save thousands of American
lives next year by simply pulling out of Vietnam tomorrow.
But this is just as impossible as abolishing automobiles—which
take many more lives each year. Maybe this sort of double-
think, saying one thing but living by something else, is what
drives the hippies and flower children up the wall.

It's time to sweep out a lot of this peace-at-any-price and
rather-Red-than-dead rubbish, and to reaffirm some of the
old "corny" ideas that helped to make the country great. One
of them was that we must be ready to die in defense of the
country.

Unless this country has got something that is worth dying
for, and unless we are willing to die for it, it won't remain
great much longer. And it won't deserve to!

One rather shocking way to explain the *Pueblo*'s surrender
without a fight is to say that they just didn't think that this
country was worth fighting for. I doubt that anyone on the
Pueblo felt that way on the afternoon of the surrender. But
maybe a week later, they did.

At any rate, when the *Pueblo* sent her SOS, we didn't
think *they* were worth fighting for. Several of the *Pueblo*
crew have testified that they fully expected this country to
react fast and forcibly to save them and that they were
perfectly willing to accept whatever happened to them in a
fight to get them back. They were amazed, and ashamed,
when we made no move to help them.

True, their own skipper had surrendered them without
firing a shot—to save them from "certain" slaughter. No good

military commander leads his men to certain death in a hopeless cause, and Bucher says he thought this was hopeless.

But few things are certain on this earth, and lost causes sometimes have been turned into glorious victories, although if you surrender without firing a shot, you will never know what might have happened if you had fought.

Back in 1779, when the captain of H.M.S. *Serapis* hailed John Paul Jones and asked, "Have you struck your colors, sir?" the U.S.S. *Bonne Homme Richard* was a battered, water-logged hulk, dismasted and burning. Jones had plenty of reason to answer, "I surrender." But he answered otherwise—and fought on to board and capture the *Serapis*.

If George Washington had valued human life above everything else, he would have run up a white flag at Valley Forge, and there would be no U.S.A. today.

In World War II, in the Battle of the Bulge, the Germans had General McAuliffe's outfit surrounded and apparently all set up for the kill. When they asked McAuliffe, "Are you ready to surrender?" his reply might well have been, "Affirmative." Instead, it was, "Nuts."

In each of these cases bright pages were written into our history books. Each had its price in human lives. Was it worth the price? I think so.

There is a verse in Macaulay's poem, *Horatius at the Bridge*, that answers this question about the value of life better than anything else I know. The Etruscan army is bearing down on Rome and the Romans are trying frantically to destroy the last bridge over the Tiber before they get there. The vanguard of the invaders is in sight, and it looks like the Romans won't get the bridge down in time. They call for volunteers to fight at the far end of the bridge and hold the invaders up long enough for them to finish the job. It looks like a suicide mission for anyone who volunteers—and for a moment, no one does. Then Horatius steps forward.

> Then out spake brave Horatius,
> The Captain of the Gate:
> "To every man upon this earth
> Death cometh soon or late;
> And how can man die better
> Than facing fearful odds
> For the ashes of his fathers
> And the temples of his gods?"

Admiral Arleigh Burke tells of an incident during the Okinawa invasion when he was Admiral Mitscher's Chief of Staff on the *Bunker Hill*. The kamikazes were giving us a bad time then, and our destroyers far out on the radar picket line were catching hell.

Sometimes freak atmospheric conditions carried voice radio transmissions way beyond their normal range to the horizon. One morning on the *Bunker Hill's* flag bridge, the TBS (talk between ships) loudspeaker picked up a destroyer on the picket line over a hundred miles away.

"Songbird to Eagle—Songbird to Eagle—URGENT. Ensign Jones talking—we just took a kamikaze on the bridge—it's real bad—others coming—captain and exec dead—I think I'm the only officer left— . . . I've only been in this Navy a little while, so if I do anything wrong, that's why—but I'm going to fight this ship as long as she stays afloat—Songbird out."

There was a dead silence on the bridge of the *Bunker Hill*. Everyone was too choked up to say anything. Mitscher, Burke, and the others just glared at each other defiantly—and proudly —and went on about their business.

That's how it used to be—only twenty-five years ago.

8. NATIONAL CHARACTER

After we point an accusing finger at everyone who had anything to do with the *Pueblo,* we still haven't finished the messy job of fixing all the blame. This is a national disgrace that goes beyond the mistakes or omissions of Bucher, the admirals, and the Secretary of Defense.

We all share the blame, and the *Pueblo* is an ominous symptom of decay in our national character. The real cause of the fiasco is our present way of life, the false values we are adopting and our cynical attitude toward the old-fashioned virtues that made this country great.

The virtues of our pioneer ancestors are now regarded as "corny"—for squares only. Thrift, hard work, and self-reliance are for the birds. This is the Great Society, in which security is the main objective in life, and everyone is entitled to free lunch off the government even if they are too lazy to work for it. Honesty? This is the era of phony expense accounts, tax loopholes, and Bobby Baker wheelers and dealers. Patriotism? Burn your draft cards, run Marine recruiters off the campus, and make heroes of deserters who find refuge in Sweden.

We tolerate all sorts of lawlessness by racial groups, screwball students, and gangster-ridden unions striking against the public interest. The way to get what you want, these days, is to simply have enough muscle to take it, regardless of the law. The Supreme Court encourages this by protecting the rights of criminals so zealously that law-abiding citizens are losing their right to be protected from criminals. The Court itself sets an example in flouting law and order by illegally amending the Constitution and making new laws by a five-to-four vote.

We are becoming a nation of phonies. What you *are* doesn't matter much—it's your public image that counts. You can be the worst crook that ever cheated a widow out of her pittance, but if you've got a good public relations man who can project the right image for you, you've got it made. Make a big enough splash to get on the cover of *Time* or *Life* and be featured in living color on TV, and it doesn't matter what you did to make the splash. You have become a Very Important Person.

When the *Pueblo*'s men were brought back to the United States, their arrival was featured on nationwide TV and they were hailed as conquering heroes. While a prisoner, the *Pueblo*'s skipper, Commander Bucher, was made an honorary citizen of Pueblo, Arizona. Upon his return, the town gave him a triumphal welcome and civic reception. Proposals have been made to award medals to all men in his crew.

Shortly after their return to the United States *Parade* magazine (circulation fourteen million weekly) had Bucher's picture on the cover and a long story about the fabulous offers he was getting to cash in on his publicity. *Parade* said he was the best-known officer in the U. S. Navy and should make a bundle from book rights, TV, and the movies—maybe two million dollars or more. Various big-time publishers competed for his story and a number of ghost writers scrambled for the job of writing it.

This brings to mind the way they used to pay off the crew of the old whaling ships. Nobody drew any regular pay, but at the end of a voyage when the oil was sold everybody got a share of the profit. The captain, the mate, and the harpooners got the biggest shares, but everybody got some, the amount depending on his job. I think perhaps Bucher might want to split the swag with his crew that way if he cashes in.

Isn't that a revealing sidelight on what has happened to our sense of values? This is the country of George Washington, Nathan Hale, John Paul Jones, etc., etc.

Anywhere in the United States today, a Congressional Medal of Honor will get you a cup of coffee—if you have 15 cents to go with it. But surrendering your ship without a fight can get you fame and fortune.

I wonder how the astronauts feel about that? Their literary rights are pretty tightly tied up. I wonder how the GIs out in the jungles of Vietnam feel about it?

The young lads who are entering the Army, Navy, Air Force, and Marines now have grown up in this atmosphere. How can you expect them to take any stock in such stuff as: "I have not yet begun to fight"—"Don't give up the ship"—and "I regret I have only one life to give for my country"?

Bucher was brought up in Boys Town, Nebraska, the orphans home made famous by Father Flannigan. It used to send out a wonderful Christmas card showing a kid carrying a smaller one piggyback through the snow and saying, "He ain't heavy, Father—*he's* my brother." I am sure the good fathers there taught the kids all the old-fashioned virtues.

But the world the kids grew up in is down-grading these

virtues. Its heroes are not in the history books. They are on the TV programs and the front pages—and you don't make those spots by helping old ladies to cross the street.

Bucher and his men are products of their times and are no different from their contemporaries. It is absurd to try to pin the blame for their conduct on any one individual. The blame belongs to the whole country. Our way of life has produced a generation of sailors and officers who surrender without a fight, and millions of Americans applaud them for it!

A *Pueblo* affair would have been unthinkable only twenty years ago. Now, we not only condone it; we try to make something heroic out of it. We have become so used to contempt for the law at home that we can't get excited about it on the high seas. Many bearded oddballs defy the authority of the U. S. Government at home and get away with it. Why make a federal case out of a bunch of gooks doing it on the other side of the world in the Sea of Japan?

It seems that a part of our way of life these days is that everybody has to have some sort of a guilt complex. We feel guilty because our ancestors persecuted the Negroes and robbed the Indians. We feel guilty because Hitler slaughtered the Jews. Many of us who have never been hungry feel guilty because a lot of people in this world are hungry. The *Pueblo* gives us all a fine chance to wallow in guilt.

Personally, I can't work up much of a guilty feeling about any of the other things mentioned above. I had nothing to do with them. But I can work up a hell of a feeling of guilt about the *Pueblo*. I served forty-three years in the U. S. Navy, and it was a wonderful outfit when I joined it. I certainly can't take any pride in seeing it go to pot in my lifetime. I hope I can get enough others to feel that way while there is still time left to save it.

I am sixty-eight years old now, and don't expect to be around much longer. I've got no axes to grind and can say what I think without caring whose feathers I ruffle. I'm bound to ruffle a lot of them, because it becomes more obvious every day that hardly anyone agrees with me now except maybe some old-fashioned fuddy-duds like myself. If that is the public image I project—so be it. I'm glad I wasn't born thirty years later than I was, and that I am behind the present times. I hope I'm not still around to say "I told you so" when the death agony of the country sets in. I certainly don't want to be here for the funeral.

One of the warning signposts on the downhill road of other great empires, like Rome and Greece, has been the decline in public morals as shown in their art and literature. This sign is quite clear in this country now. Perhaps the greatest force for molding our thinking today is TV. Just look at the fare that's served up daily on the TV networks—crime and violence all over the dial. Day after day, our youngsters sit in front of the tube learning what it's like in the grown-ups' world. The networks put out what the grown-ups like because that's how they peddle their advertising. What the grown-ups like is violence. How can you expect our youngsters to have any respect for law and order after they grow up when they are raised on a daily diet of contempt for it—approved by their parents?

Music is supposed to be one of the higher forms of art. Listen, if you can stand it, to the popular music of today. A bunch of long-haired, bearded youths of indeterminate sex twang on queer-shaped guitars, holler, make faces, and twist their butts around. This is supposed to be music. They sell millions of records, are featured on the "Ed Sullivan Show" and are mobbed by screaming fans wherever they go. If you don't dig them, you're square.

Perhaps the worst sign of decline in national character is in our literature. Pornography has become an art, and Big Business. The most shocking part of this is that the principal promoter and champion of pornography is the U. S. Supreme Court, which defends it as essential to free speech. The Court says it's illegal to yell "fire" in a crowded theater, but free speech demands that we allow smut peddlers to deluge the minds of our kids with filth.

I had a brush a few years ago in court with the smut peddlers. There was a trial involving a notoriously obscene and filthy book, in which the defense brought in some long-haired English professors from the University of Maryland to testify that the book had literary merit. I'm no professor, but I have written more books than any of the longhairs had, so the state called me as an expert to say the book had no merit.

I was asked, "What is the philosophy of life expressed by this book?"

I asked the judge if I could answer using the language of the book. This, of course, put the other side on the spot, because they couldn't very well object and say, "Oh no, your Honor—you can't allow *that* kind of language in court." His Honor said "O.K.—go ahead."

My reply was, "It is the philosophy of a cur dog, namely, if you can't eat it or fuck it—piss on it."

I feel that this accurately sums up much of the best-selling "literature" of our times. One of our leading publishers has just brought out a new book called *Portnoy's Complaint*. This book got the greatest advance ballyhoo of any book I can recall. All the "liberal" critics had orgasms over it and gave it extravagant praise . . . "most significant book of our times" . . . "landmark in the history of current literature" . . . "a masterpiece such as you see once in a lifetime." You would have a right to think from all this that this was a book of great historical importance, or drove home some great moral lesson, or perhaps told some simple story in a remarkably beautiful way.

Actually, the book is a bucket of shit. Every page of it is fouled with obscene four-letter words. I don't object to these words when they are needed to express a worth-while idea. But the ideas in this book are all filthy and obscene. Even if you used proper dictionary words in place of all the gutter words, it would still be a foul book, because the whole theme of it is obscene. Just the same, the week it came out it zoomed to the top of the best-seller lists.

Since retiring from the Navy, I have had pretty good luck as a scribbler and have written seven books. But I'm afraid that later on, it may embarrass my grandchildren to know about this. It might be better to tell them that after forty-three years in the Navy, Granddaddy retired and got a job playing the piano in a high-class whore house.

If you ask me, "What does all this have to do with the *Pueblo?*" my answer is, "It has a great deal to do with it. It is a chilling warning of the decline in national character, which is the basic reason for such things as the *Pueblo.*"

We had better heed this warning before we pass the point of no return. If anyone had predicted ten years ago that law and order would collapse in this country as it is doing today, he would have been put in the booby hatch.

Just look at our universities. A rabble of hoodlums takes over the dean's office in Columbia and uses it as a privy. When the dean finally calls the cops and they crack a few skulls throwing the young pigs out, people are shocked—not at what the pigs did, but at the fact that the cops didn't handle them with tender, loving care! It's spreading all over the land—Harvard, Colgate, Cornell—each day the list gets longer. If things keep on as they are going, in another ten years the whole U.S.A. will be one big booby hatch.

One reason for the trouble with our youth is that we have skimmed several million of our best young men off into the armed services. So the riffraff and scum are surfacing and taking over, while the cream of the crop are busy defending the freedom of the hippies and queers to raise any kind of hell they see fit.

In Chicago, during the convention, the city was poised on the brink of a bloody race riot. Firm action by the mayor and the police averted a shambles in which many would have been killed and a large section of the city burned down. This was done without firing a shot and with no serious injuries, although the police had to rough up a number of goons, a lot of misguided hippies, and some reporters trying to stir up headlines by making trouble. The press and TV are still screaming police brutality. But what promised to be the worst race riot in our history didn't come off.

Crime is skyrocketing all over the country, and the police are handcuffed by the courts in trying to control it. The courts, featherbedding for their legal colleagues, are more zealous of protecting the rights of the clients of criminal lawyers than they are of protecting citizens who don't need lawyers. Hoodlums trample all over the rights of ordinary citizens, but can always find plenty of do-gooders to defend their "rights" for them if they ever fall afoul of the law.

If the sort of things that are happening in this country today took place in Russia or Red China, we would be very smug about it. We would say, with good reason, "They can't last much longer."

All this has a direct bearing on the *Pueblo* case. The crew of the *Pueblo* are the product of the times we are living in. They are all young men, who have grown up in a permissive and submissive society where illegal use of force is tolerated and condoned. They are accustomed to seeing hoodlums, the Mafia, and mobs prevail over the law at home. They saw nothing very wrong in submitting to piracy on the high seas.

The reaction of the country to this was cut from the same cloth. We are afraid to use force at home (police brutality!), so why use it abroad? Greet the boys as heroes when they get home.

Of course, we are presently using quite a lot of force in Vietnam. But—

A foolish consistency is the hobgoblin of little minds,
adored by little statesmen and philosophers and divines.

The majority of our statesmen, philosophers, and divines as well as a queer assortment of eggheads and hippies seem to approve of what we did, or rather didn't do, in the *Pueblo* case.

So, at the cost of national humiliation, we *perhaps* saved the lives of eighty-two of our men who might—or might not—have been killed by savages if they had reacted the way Americans always have before, when our honor was at stake.

I wonder what these men will do now that they are home again safe and sound to help preserve their country from the things that are threatening to destroy it.

Public reaction to this thing, as reflected by press, radio, and TV is grave warning as to how far the country has drifted from the ideals that made it great. When an outrage like piracy is committed against a strong country, you might expect the main reaction of that country's press would be indignation at the pirates and demand for satisfaction. But in the *Pueblo* case, the makers of public opinion have gone overboard whipping up sympathy for Bucher and his men. This produced some fine sob stories, which were great for circulation but no good for the future of the country. This pitch went over so big that there is now serious talk of giving medals to this crew which surrendered without a fight.

Less than twenty-five years ago at the end of World War II, a *Pueblo* incident would have been impossible. Now, all the sob sisters of press, radio, and TV are defending the abject surrender of the ship. At the end of World War II, if the officers had given up control of the ship, some of the sailors would have fought on anyway. I speak from intimate firsthand knowledge of our sailors at that time. Now, all of

Bucher's men praise his decision to surrender and say they would be glad to serve under his command again. I fully approve of a crew being loyal to their skipper. But—the fact that they all feel as they do is an ominous sign of the times. God knows what we can expect twenty years from now!

After the Korean War there was a scandal about American prisoners who were brainwashed and tortured into collaborating with the enemy and, in some cases, selling out their buddies to get special privileges. But there were quite a number of good Americans who took all the gooks could dish out and didn't break. They wouldn't surrender even under torture as prisoners. None of these men got any medals for refusing to surrender. I have heard some bitter comments about this medal bit from wives of men who are now prisoners of the Viet Cong. They say they would like to write the citations!

The press have also had a Roman holiday in the *Pueblo* case blasting one of their favorite targets, the military brass. Ever since the end of World War II, the press and the long-haired literary eggheads have done a masterful hatchet job on the brass.

When I was young, a brass hat with gold braid on the visor was an honorable status symbol, respected everywhere in the country. Now, in many circles it calls for an apologetic explanation from the wearer. "General" and "admiral" have become almost dirty words. There are riots on college campuses now demanding abolition of the ROTC.

The hatchet job done on the brass has been so effective that generals and admirals no longer run the Army, Navy, and Air Force. This is done by bright-eyed young management experts of the Defense Department who haven't been corrupted by military service. The generals and admirals are responsible only for the nuts and bolts, if they can justify them as being cost effective. This comes under the heading of Civilian Control of the Military, which has become a sacred cow of the longhairs.

"Military-industrial complex" is another shibboleth which is supposed to expose a Bad Thing. But this complex is what has built a national defense for this country capable of protecting it from foreign aggression—anywhere except off the coast of Korea. This defense enables the longhairs to conduct riots in the streets and college campuses without fear of interference by any foreign government (to say nothing of our own). I think the liberals of Hungary and Czechoslovakia would have been grateful had they had a similar military-industrial complex in their hours of need!

But the brass are still the whipping boys who have to take the rap when the young global strategists of the Pentagon think tanks goof. In the *Pueblo* case the brass has much to answer for, and the press, always alert to espouse a popular cause that will help to sell advertising, has been smiting them hip and thigh. But the press has said nothing about the biggest fault that can properly be charged to the brass— namely, allowing eager amateurs to usurp the job of running the military defense of the country. The brass are supposed to be experts at defending the country against foreign invasion. But they turned out to be rank amateurs at defending themselves from the whiz kids!

In reporting the *Pueblo* case, the press, radio, and TV have, as usual, been more concerned with making a big splurge than with telling the facts. An example of this is the way they all handled the Navy court of inquiry's warning to Bucher about his legal rights. Early in his testimony, Bucher admitted that he surrendered his ship without a fight. This, of course, is an offense against federal law, for which a naval officer can be court-martialed. The senior member of the court was required by law to remind Bucher at this point of his right under the Fifth Amendment of refusing to say any more on the grounds that he might incriminate himself. This is one of many legal rights of lawbreakers so zealously protected by our great bulwark of law and order, the Supreme Court. The Navy court simply recognized that these rights apply also even to naval officers, and did what the law required it to do. Of course, the taxpayers have a right to know why a naval officer surrenders one of their ships without a fight, and in deference to that right, Bucher waived his right to remain silent.

This routine warning generated headlines all over the country, "Navy Threatens Bucher with Court-Martial." This was twisting the facts to make a headline, and even newspaper editors are smart enough to know this. But a headline, "Navy Informs Bucher of Constitutional Rights," doesn't help to increase circulation and sell advertising. "Navy Threatens to Court-Martial Bucher" does.

If any civil court in the country failed to warn a murderer of the many legal rights, dodges, and quibbles to which he is entitled, all the lawyers and liberal sob sisters in the country would be up in arms. In a murder trial nowadays, the first question is not, "Is the prisoner actually the man who hit the old lady with the ax and buried her body in the woods?" It is, "How did the cops find out about this?" If they asked the prisoner some shrewd questions, or if his mouthpiece wasn't at his elbow when they made the pinch, or if they tapped his telephone, the whole case goes down the drain. But when a naval court warns a witness, sloppy reporting raises the cry, "Navy Threatens Bucher," and these same sob sisters get indignant about "the brass" trying to cashier this heroic young officer.

The Chief of Naval Operations, Admiral Moorer, finally had to make a special statement about this to set the record straight. But, as is always the case, this statement got perhaps one-tenth as much space in the press as the original slanted stories did.

Bucher, of course, chose to waive his rights and told the whole story, as any naval officer would. If he had availed himself of the rights that we extend to any hoodlum and clammed up, we would never have known just how the *Pueblo* surrender came about . . . unless, of course, we were able to get the North Koreans to come into court to tell about it.

This last idea is not as farfetched as it may sound. Government lawyers did something very much like that right after World War II. The U.S.S. *Indianapolis* was sunk by a Japanese submarine just as the war ended, and her crew swam around in the middle of the Pacific for several days before anyone knew she was missing. There was a big scandal and a public clamor to crucify the brass. So the captain was court-martialed for losing his ship. Believe it or not, one of the witnesses called by the U. S. Government at this court-martial was the skipper of the Japanese submarine that sank *Indianapolis!*

The lawyers have been muscling in on running the military services, just like the whiz kids have. They now have the administration of justice by military courts handcuffed almost as badly as it is in the civil courts. This process began right after World War II, when the lawyers joined the general attack on the brass and got Congress to overhaul the whole system of military justice. In general, the old system had worked well, military men got a square deal, and discipline in the services was good—good enough to win all the wars fought under the old legal codes. But they uncovered a few mistakes and abuses under the old system—as there will be under any system run by human beings. The lawyers raised such a whoop-de-do over the worms they uncovered that Congress burned down the barn to get rid of a few rats, and set up the new Uniform Code of Military Justice.

One of the main features of the new code is that it is too complicated to be run by military men. It takes a whole lot of lawyers to do business under it, and so it created a lot of nice new jobs for lawyers in the military services. Now, lawyers can make a career in the service and get to be colonels, generals, and admirals. And now, a skipper can't even bawl out a lubberly seaman unless the sailor has the ship's legal beagle at his elbow, advising him of his rights.

A court-martial has become such a cumbersome thing, and such a pain in the neck to the command that convenes it, that no one will convene a court now if there is any way of getting around it. The easiest way around it usually is "administrative procedure"—meaning an undesirable discharge. This sort of discharge is meant for misfits and ne'er-do-wells who just can't adjust to military service, not for real bad actors. But to try a bad actor by court-martial and give him proper punishment is just as hard as trying to convict a hoodlum in civil court. If the services tried to court-martial the small percentage of bad actors who deserve it, they wouldn't have time to train the good men to defend the country.

The services thus now have a choice of two evils: (1) they can let a lot of serious crimes go unpunished, or (2) they can get so involved in legal proceedings that they can't do their main job of protecting the country. They choose ✕1 as the lesser evil, and any bad actor who wants out can get out pretty easily. This is why the desertion rate is skyrocketing in such a shocking manner, and why the court-martial rate for desertion is so low.

While the *Pueblo* court of inquiry was in session, a committee of Congress was investigating the desertion rate in the

Armed Services. This committee produced shocking figures on desertions—fifty thousand in 1968; ten thousand more than in 1967.

This figure alone is a grim indication of the decay in national character now infecting the country. It helps explain why a Navy ship will surrender without firing a shot and the vast majority of our citizens will approve.

But the press took little notice of this symptom of national sickness. It did, however, wax indignant at the brass over a minor incident uncovered in this investigation.

Over a year ago, a group of men deserted from our Army in Germany and took refuge in Sweden. These men were welcomed by hippie groups in Sweden and made a big anti-U.S. splurge in press, radio, and TV. But after the splurge, they found that the food they were being given by the Swedes wasn't as good as the Army chow they were accustomed to. One of them finally came back to the United States and gave himself up. The Army court-martialed him for desertion and sentenced him to four years at hard labor.

Immediately all the sob sisters put up a howl. They said, "How can you expect the other defectors in Sweden to come back when you treat this poor fellow that way?"

The answer of course is, "Who the hell *wants* them back? The Swedes welcomed them with open arms and helped them to spread their anti-U.S. poison. Let the Swedes keep 'em."

Another newsworthy angle of this desertion story, neglected by the press, is the scandalously low court-martial rate for deserters. Desertion is a very serious crime against the United States, bordering on treason. Only about 1 per cent of these quitters are ever tried by court-martial. The rest are handled by "administrative procedures." This is Pentagon gobbledegook for "the easiest way out."

The reason for this sad state of affairs is the same one that is clogging up our civilian courts and making a farce out of law enforcement, namely, undue emphasis on the legal rights of criminals. Military courts are now just as handcuffed as civilian courts are in trying to deal with lawbreakers.

Even so, when we do crack down, as in the Swedish case, the press and liberals all clamor against the brass. If the Navy attempted to court-martial Bucher for surrendering without a fight in violation of Article 0730 and federal law, I think nearly any good lawyer could beat the rap for him under the present system. And judging from the opinion polls that have appeared on the subject, a court-martial for Bucher would be a worse disaster for the Navy's public image than Pearl Harbor. I'm afraid that as of A.D. 1969 we just have to accept the fact that all that the U.S. public expects of a Navy skipper, when the going looks real tough, is surrender without a fight. In fact, one of the frightening aspects of this case is that if the Navy *did* decide to court-martial Bucher, a court composed of the rising generation of naval officers *might* acquit him!

An example of the kind of legal hocus-pocus the services now have to contend with came up early in the Navy's *Pueblo* inquiry. The question was, did the *Pueblo*'s crew violate the Code of Conduct by signing false confessions while imprisoned, and should they therefore be warned about their legal rights, as Bucher was.

The Code of Conduct was promulgated by executive order of the President and says, "By virtue of the authority vested in me as President of the United States and as Commander in Chief of the Armed Forces of the United States, I hereby prescribe the Code of Conduct for Members of the Armed Forces of the United States, which is attached to this order and made a part hereof . . ." etc., etc.

Article V of this Code reads, "When questioned, should I become a prisoner of war, I am bound to give only name, rank, serial number, and date of birth. I will evade answering further questions to the utmost of my ability. I will make no oral or written statements disloyal to my country and its allies or to their cause."

This sounds pretty official and binding to me. It seems to confront the lawyers with the task of court-martialing the *Pueblo* men who signed false confessions, a task which would be extremely unpopular. But they squirmed out of it very handily. They ruled that the Code applies only to prisoners of war and these men were not POWs—they were "illegal detainees." This sounds like a Philadelphia lawyer at his pettifogging best. It shows that lawyers are lawyers, even if you put a blue uniform on them and give them brass hats.

Then someone pointed out that the gooks used this same line of reasoning to justify their mistreatment of the *Pueblo*'s crew; i.e.—they were not POWs who came under the Geneva Convention; they were spies.

So, on further thought, the lawyers reversed themselves and said the code did apply to the *Pueblo*'s men, but that there was no legal penalty for violating it. It was simply an ideal toward which we should strive—like the Ten Commandments.

When I learned the Ten Commandments I was told that a rather severe penalty eventually was attached to violating them. Of course, those who don't believe in this penalty don't take the Ten Commandments very seriously either. But it seems to me an executive order from the President should be taken very seriously indeed by members of our Armed Forces.

Be that as it may, the lawyers want no part of trying the *Pueblo*'s men for violating the Code. It's hard enough to convict a wrongdoer of anything these days in a court-martial. It would be ridiculous to try to convict the *Pueblo* boys after the way the United States itself signed a false confession to bail them out of imprisonment. And a trial that resulted in an acquittal would make the Code even more of a dead letter than it is now.

Another false charge leveled at the brass by snipers in the press is that the Navy is prejudiced against Bucher because he is not an Academy man. This is a low blow, as any good reporter can easily find out. If this were true, the Navy would be prejudiced against most of its officers these days. Of all the new ensigns commissioned in the Navy last year, only one out of eighteen is a Naval Academy man. The Navy officers' corps becomes more and more civilian-educated every year, and can't survive without the annual input from NROTC. This source of officers is now under attack by the same long-hairs who love to lambaste the brass, and several leading Ivy League colleges have recently run recruiting teams off the campus and stopped credit for NROTC work.

The Navy is having great trouble now persuading young officers to stay in at the end of their obligated service and make a career of the Navy. Bucher is one of the few who did. The fact that he had a perfectly normal career up to the *Pueblo* business and was promoted to commander just as fast as his Annapolis contemporaries is clear proof that there was no prejudice against him because of his background.

The trouble we are having getting career officers bodes ill for the Navy of the future. The trouble is due in large measure to the constant sniping at the brass and denigrating of the professional officers by press, radio, TV, and the literary community. Navy pay has never been any real inducement to career men, and sea duty has always taken officers away from home for long periods. But in former days, a naval officer had some status in the community and could look forward to responsible jobs as he advanced in rank. Now he is looked on as a second-class citizen by many, and more and more as he advances in rank, he is taking orders from whiz kids.

Thus the two big incentives that used to keep officers in the Navy are disappearing. If the present trend continues, the Navy will see no more Ernie Kings, Halseys, Nimitzes, Arleigh Burkes, or George Andersons.

One of the outstanding facts of life in the year of A.D. 1969 is that the two greatest countries in the world are devoting a lion's share of their total national effort into producing systems of mutual annihilation, which can only justify their existence by never being used. All reasonable men know that this is an insane way to keep the peace. But human nature being what it is, and the state of the world being what it is in 1969, the only thing that would be more insane would be for either side to scrap its weapons unilaterally and hope the other side would do likewise.

Peace is a great blessing, and we can have it in either one of two ways—both of them expensive. We can keep ready to defend ourselves, and the cost of this is about one hundred billion a year. Or we can simply submit to the Communists—and the price of this is slavery.

The *Pueblo* affair is grim proof of how totally incompatible our ideas of good and evil are with those of the Communists. Our basic standards of value are as far apart as the North and South poles of the earth. Black and white, right and wrong can't compromise and still be what they were before. It's a sad comment on our civilization, but this is why the only thing that makes mutual coexistence possible is the threat of instant mutual extermination.

The capture of the *Pueblo* is one example of how far apart our standards are. Piracy on the high seas is simply unthinkable to the Western mind. Even the tough-minded JCS didn't give it serious thought when weighing the risks of *Pueblo*'s mission. But to the gooks, right and wrong don't mean a thing —piracy is perfectly O.K., if you can get away with it.

The "confession" that the United States signed to obtain release of *Pueblo*'s crew is another stark example of our different moral values. On our side of the iron curtain, a coerced confession is of no value. We go to great lengths to protect habitual criminals from confessions that fail to meet a long array of technicalities, even when every word in them is true.

In the *Pueblo* confession, General Woodward, the official representative of the United States, said publicly to the gooks before signing, "This is a lot of rubbish. It is not true. I am signing it only to obtain release of our men." Thus he affixed his signature on behalf of the United States, while the gooks grinned their approval.

To us, this whole business was fartial. To the gooks, it produced a perfectly good and useful confession.

The Russians seem to understand our fear of nuclear war better than we do theirs. Fear of starting something that could escalate into nuclear doesn't deter them from overrunning Hungary and Czechoslovakia. But it stops us from rescuing our own ship when it is boarded by pirates.

In trying to control the bomb, we've got a wild bull by the tail, and this affects everything else we do. Fear that an incident on the other side of the world could escalate into an atomic war is so great that Washington restricts field commanders' freedom to act more and more and is taking over actual command of everything. Generals and admirals are, therefore, reluctant to act, and are prone to refer any unusual decision to Washington. This is as it should be if there is real danger of escalation. But human nature being what it is, this means that many things are referred to Washington when there is no real danger of escalation. This often means that no decision at all is made until it is too late—which is exactly what happened in the case of the *Pueblo*.

In this affair we got a dose, on the high seas, of the kind of brute force and lawlessness that we have learned to accept meekly on our streets and college campuses at home. We are becoming a permissive and submissive society in which small but violent minorities run roughshod over the law. We tolerate and condone flagrant lawlessness by racial groups, screwball students, draft card burners, and unions striking against the public interest. The way to get what you want in this country today is to simply bring enough muscle to bear to take it. Any attempt to maintain law and order against a violent minority is met with screams of police brutality and violation of constitutional rights.

This permissive frame of mind now extends to our relations with other nations. Even though we are the most powerful country in the world, we submit to outrageous violations of international law. We have overwhelming force in the atom bomb, which of course we can't use, except as a suicidal last resort. We also have overwhelming conventional force, which we are afraid to use lest it escalate into atomic war. The frustrating fact is we are so powerful we are afraid to use our strength. At home, the police and National Guard could quickly restore order if we told them to. But we are afraid to let them use force. In Vietnam, trying to pass on the blessings of our way of life to a backward people, we get sucked into a gradually escalating war where our aim seems to be to just barely win it. As a result, it turns out to be a no-win war.

The *Pueblo* is a classic example of what this permissive attitude leads to. The same frame of mind that tolerates flagrant lawlessness at home now makes it possible for small outlaw countries to ride roughshod over international law and get away with piracy on the high seas against our Navy ships.

Less than twenty-five years ago, the United States had the most powerful Army, Navy, and Air Force on this earth and knew how to use them. Our terms to Germany and Japan were "Unconditional Surrender." Now, we've still got great power, but we no longer know how to use it. After thrashing around for eight years in Vietnam and losing thirty-five thousand killed, we have finally got the gooks to agree to the size and shape of a table in Paris.

Putting it bluntly, this is what Mr. McNamara, with his scientific business methods and handcuffing of field commanders, has done to our Armed Forces. Now we can just about hold our own against third-rate Asiatic powers.

Much bigger and more ominous examples of this than the *Pueblo* are the two wars that this country has fought since Unification came into being. Under the old system, we fought seven major wars between George Washington's time and 1945—and won them all. In the last one before Unification, we smashed the Nazi-Jap alliance, the greatest military combine the world had ever seen up to that time. Since Unification, we have fought two wars against third-rate Asiatic powers. The Korean War ended in a humiliating armistice, observed more or less by the gooks until the *Pueblo* affair. The outcome of Vietnam is still in doubt.

This country is becoming soft, just as Rome did before its decline and fall.

In 1969 it is still a great country, one that is worth preserving and keeping great. But we don't do it if all we ask of our Armed Forces is surrender without a fight when the going gets tough.

There are worse things than dying for your country. Many Hungarians and Czechs can testify that if you won't fight for your country, it may not be worth living in.

This was an accepted fact of life to our ancestors. If we are to preserve the country that they left to us, we have got to keep this idea alive in our children.

There is little indication so far that anything will come out of the *Pueblo* incident to do this. The report of the Navy's court of inquiry and the high command's action on it has now been published. The inquiry recommended general court-martial for Bucher and Lieutenant Harris and letters of reprimand for Bucher's executive, for Rear Admiral Johnson, and for his Chief of Staff of Intelligence. CINCPAC and CNO decided against any court-martial and recommended letters of reprimand instead. The Secretary of the Navy, exercising his civilian control, decided there would be no disciplinary action whatever. (See appendix E)

This is all right—as far as it goes. The Secretary was rather mealymouthed in failing to condemn Bucher's surrender without a fight. But he is a lawyer surrounded by military lawyers so you could hardly expect him to make a forthright statement about a difficult case. The professional Navy, at least, took a hard-nosed view of it.

In assessing blame the court of inquiry stopped at a low level in the chain of command. The Secretary touched gingerly on the question of high-level responsibility. He says, "the charges against Rear Admiral Johnson relate to the failure to anticipate the emergency that subsequently developed. This basic accusation, however, could be leveled in various degrees

at responsible superior authorities in the chain of command
and control in the support structure."

This is a very light brushoff indeed for the many serious
failures all the way up the chain of command. But if that
winds up the *Pueblo* case as far as the Navy is concerned, at
least one big question is left unanswered: Why didn't the
Enterprise do something on the afternoon of the capture? The
Navy's need for carriers is coming under heavy attack now
with big budget cuts in the offing and the Navy may be badly
embarrassed later by its failure to give a frank answer to this
question.

The Secretary's action touches only briefly on the Code of
Conduct. He says, "The Court was of the opinion that during
his internment Commander Bucher upheld morale in a
superior manner; that he provided leadership by insisting that
command structure be maintained and providing guidance for
conduct; and that he contributed to the ability of the crew to
hold together and to withstand the trials of detention until
repatriation could be effected."

That's fine. But Bucher and his men, as well as the United
States Government violated the Code by signing false confessions. This seems to make a dead letter of the Code. I feel
that Congress should take a hard look at the Code and modify
it where necessary so that both our soldiers and the country
can live up to it. Perhaps some of the ideas proposed in
Appendix A should be adopted.

Finally, the most important question raised by the *Pueblo*
affair remains to be answered. It is: What are we going to do
about the way of life that produced a generation of sailors
and officers who surrendered without a fight and millions of
citizens who applaud them for it?

That question has a vital bearing on the future of this
country. The answer to it is in the hands of people who will
be around longer than I will.

WE CAN BAFFLE THE BRAINWASHERS!
by
Rear Admiral D. V. Gallery, USN
The Saturday Evening Post, January 22, 1955, page 20

The treatment of American prisoners by the Reds in the Korean War poses the free nations an evil problem: "What can we do about the Communists' hellish brainwashing technique for torturing 'confessions' out of prisoners of war?"

This inhuman method for tampering with men's minds and souls defies all laws of God or man. It lays bare the frightful difference between our Western civilization and the godless creed of communism. The Reds used it ruthlessly on American prisoners of war in Korea, treating our men like laboratory rats in a diabolical scientific experiment.

A number of these men, through fear of being tortured to death, gave lip service to the Red creed or signed obviously false "germ-warfare confessions." Now some of them are being court-martialed or disgraced for cowardice and collaboration with the enemy.

This is happening in a country which let victory in Korea slip through its fingers because of fear—fear that we might touch off World War III, and thus get hurt ourselves. We try our soldiers for cowardice—after a war which we didn't have the guts to win!

There is an uneasy feeling in the land about these POW trials. But the trials are just a small, messy piece of the whole big problem—the piece least worthy of public sympathy. The real problem concerns the many other prisoners who took everything the Red devils could do to them and didn't break. Before we can live in good conscience with those thirty-eight hundred men the Reds let come back alive, we Americans have got to face this problem honestly and courageously.

Perhaps, if we wanted to, we could even forget the past, avoid looking our thirty-eight hundred ex-POWs in the eye, and just sweep the whole thing under the rug. But the future and the boys who haven't been captured yet make this problem cry out to heaven for solution.

I have no sympathy whatever for a prisoner who squealed on his buddies or who sold them out for his own benefit. We should throw the book at him and disgrace him. I have much sympathy for those who, under torture, gave the Reds "military information" of the kind we broadcast to the four winds in our magazines and newspapers. I understand and feel sorry for those who signed germ-warfare confessions or broadcast phony peace appeals. But the ones for whom I am really sorry are the boys who clammed up and took it, refusing to sign anything.

To be brutally frank about it, these lads accomplished nothing by their heroism. It certainly didn't bring the United States military victory. It didn't stop the Reds from winning a smashing propaganda victory in the Orient. Through the Big Lie technique they convinced the Chinese and many gullible neutrals that we were actually using germ warfare. Now our lads who held out against hellish tortures find public sympathy going to those who broke. The only good that came of their heroic resistance to brainwashing is the internal satisfaction which they themselves will feel from now on. For the rest of their lives they can look themselves in the eye when they shave in the morning and say, "Well, soldier, you took it."

As an American I am very proud of these men. But as an American I'm ashamed of the position we put them in. This must never happen again. We must fix it so that no prisoner will ever again have to endure torture to preserve the good standing of the

United States before the other free nations or will feel that an absurd confession extorted from him may be held against him if he survives.

General Dean, captured early in the Korean War, is a brave man. He got the Congressional Medal of Honor. He was never actually brainwashed, but when threatened with it, he decided the only way he could prevent the Reds from getting what they wanted out of him was suicide.

We've got to find some better choice for the defenders of our freedoms than torture, suicide, or disgrace. That's all we give them now by our rigid insistence on the Geneva Convention formula. Our military regulations say that a prisoner may state his "name, rank, and serial number," but beyond that he must clam up and endure whatever ungodly tortures the Communist devils inflict on him. As far as the regulations go, anything more can bring public disgrace when and if he ever gets home. This harsh rule is uncivilized, un-American, and stupid. It plays right into the Communists' hands, lending credibility to the few confessions which they are able to extort by brainwashing.

All through the whole stinking record of brainwashing in Korea, one thing stands out like a sore thumb: What the Reds were after was propaganda, such as germ-warfare confessions and peace appeals. Any military information they picked up was an incidental by-product. Propaganda was their real pay dirt, and it was to work this lode that they used brainwashing.

Let's lay this evil thing on the page here and look at it, if your stomach is strong enough. Brainwashing is a devilish new process developed by the Russians through experiments on dogs and rats. Their psychologist, Pavlov, found that by regimenting and frustrating animals, and by constant repetition of a set of circumstances, such as ringing a bell just before feeding them, he could "condition their reflexes" so that the animal's mouth would water every time a bell rang. He discovered he could blunt their natural instincts and replace them with "conditioned reflexes" of his own choosing.

The Red brainwashers follow this same technique. They first

reduce their victim to about the status of a dog or rat. They make you live in solitary filth, deprived of all human contacts. They strip you of all human dignity and deny you food and sleep till you are nearly, but not quite, dead. Torture is used judiciously, with clinical skill. Time drags out into eternity, where you are alone with your thoughts. You become a borderline case between a human being and a rat struggling to stay alive. Then constant, interminable repetition of their ideas erodes your brain. Your senses of proportion and values get distorted. Eventually your natural instincts may be replaced, like the rat's, by conditioned reflexes.

If they keep hammering at you that it is raining outside, sooner or later you may believe it. Sometimes, if your torturers are competent, skillful operators, they can eventually lead you out into bright sunshine and you will still think it's raining. A confused and beaten man can even be convinced that the Reds are right—that we are the aggressors and they are the peace lovers.

How much of this torture anyone can take without breaking depends entirely on the individual. No one who hasn't gone through the wringer himself can say where his own breaking point might be. Those who have been broken are the only ones who know. They are the only real experts on brainwashing on this side of the iron curtain. Those who took it without breaking are charitable toward those who did. They say, "Maybe they beat those other men harder than they did me."

The men who suffer most from brainwashing are the highest type of men our civilization produces. The Reds apply pressure to both your brain and body till one or the other breaks. If it's the brain, you confess. If it's the body, you die. The better man you are, the worse you get it.

Strong physical specimens of only average will power get off easy, because they crack soon, before their bodies are irreparably damaged. If you are weak physically, but strong-willed, that's not so bad—you will die fairly quickly. But if you are strong both physically and mentally, God help you. Occasionally the Reds lose patience with a strong will and quit, so the torturers can work on more productive subjects. But Communist patience is difficult to exhaust.

Men have always been willing to die for a principle. The history of martyrdom from the early Christian days down to the present time proves that simple fear of death cannot break a strong man's will or make him deny his faith. But months of a bare, animal-like existence, with the safe haven of death near, but always just out of reach—that is something new and diabolically different. There is abundant proof that many brave men, perfectly willing to face sudden death, cannot hold out indefinitely against this fiendish half death. In any large group, there will always be a percentage, not cowards or weaklings, but just average human beings, who will eventually break and "confess" to whatever the fiends demand. When this happens, the heroic resistance of those who held out becomes a gesture of ghastly futility.

To show that the Communists break even strong characters by brainwashing, I cite three very different types of strong men they have broken. The first is Cardinal Mindszenty. Cardinals are not weak characters—they certainly are not afraid to die. But Mindszenty "confessed" in open court to what the Reds wanted. Another strong type is Colonel Schwable, United States Marine Corps. Schwable, a flier of twenty-four years' experience, was universally regarded as an outstanding officer in a corps noted for its officers. Fliers are not afraid to die. But Schwable signed a false confession to "germ warfare." A third type is the Reds' own commissars. Commissars are unprincipled and ruthless, but they are strong, tough characters. They have to be. The Reds break them too. In the Moscow purge trials, the deposed commissars sang like canary birds!

We should know by now that we aren't all heroes and what happened in Korea will happen again. We had better quit burying our heads in the sand and do something to counter it. I don't think the American people want to keep on offering their sons the choice of suicide or disgrace.

There is a simple way out of this grim mess, if we have enough vision and imagination to use it. Recall what happened in the case of Cardinal Mindszenty. Living among the Reds and knowing their methods, he foresaw they might break him, and disavowed his "confession" long before he was even arrested. His solemn disavowal and prediction of what they would do to him was published to the world before his confession. The confession, when it came as predicted, was useless for propaganda purposes. Its publication backfired on the Reds and made them look stupid. This points the way for us on the brainwashing problem.

Suppose the President of the United States were to issue an executive order to the Armed Forces right now, telling our men that, if captured by the Reds, they may sign any document the Communists want them to or appear on radio or TV programs and deliver any script the Reds hand them. Tell them they can confess that the United States poisoned Lenin and Stalin; they can call the President a capitalist, warmongering dog of Wall Street; they can broadcast peace appeals, agree to settle behind the iron curtain when the war is over, and sign long-term leases on houses in Moscow. Give the Reds anything they want for propaganda purposes and defy them to use it!

This order would be transmitted to the United Nations with a blistering statement explaining why we had to do it, and serving notice that hereafter statements of our prisoners, made to the enemy, would be a bunch of fairy stories. This statement should be accompanied by several hundred affidavits from our men who went through the brainwashing process that will stink to high heaven. Properly publicized, this could put the Reds on the defensive in their cold war with the free world. It would spotlight the inhuman atrocities of the Communists and bring out the grim fact that the Geneva Convention, which has more or less governed the warfare of civilized nations in the past, is useless in dealing with godless fiends like the Communists. We should hammer home, on the Voice of America and at the United Nations, that this convention worked after a fashion in world wars I and II, when we were fighting human beings of more or less our own background and type. Even the Japs believed in God and a future life. But now that our enemies are ruthless, godless devils, we have to release our men from Geneva Convention restrictions.

World-wide publication of such an executive order would make the Reds look ridiculous on this side of the iron curtain when and if they attempted to use brainwash "confessions" in the future. It would leave no further motive for brainwashing except sadism. I'm sure there are many sadists in the Communist ranks, but maybe the perverted sexual urges of Red interrogators will be satisfied sooner if our boys agree with their obviously false accusations.

Some people object that our disavowal won't penetrate the iron curtain, so the Reds could use these confessions to convince their own people that we were committing atrocities. They don't need them for that. They can manufacture confessions for the benefit of their own slave peoples—make them up out of whole cloth. They need "confessions" to convince gullible neutrals.

As long as we stick to the rules we had in Korea, the Communist devils, bound by no rules of God or man, will make us look stupid. What chance has a lone GI prisoner against a battery of brainwashing Communists? Look at the record in Korea. By sticking to our outmoded Geneva Convention rule under impossible conditions, we let the Reds persuade millions that we had flouted all civilized rules and used germ warfare.

The germ-warfare charge was an easy bill of goods to sell in Korea and China, where many diseases are epidemic. What could be simpler than to blame them on United States germ bombs, producing many actual victims of the diseases to prove it? They didn't need actual confessions to do this; they could have manufactured the signatures as well as the confessions. Behind the iron curtain it made no difference whether Colonel Schwable actually wrote his confession or whether the commissars simply announced that he did. Slave peoples have no choice but to believe.

Their reason for wanting actual confessions was so they could publicize them, transmitting them to the United Nations, to raise doubts in the minds of our timid neutral friends. They succeeded in this diabolically well. They used the very organization that the free nations have set up to preserve peace and foster under-standing among nations to spread lies about us and stir up distrust and hate. From a purely technical point of view, as a propaganda operation, it was a slick job.

In propaganda the Reds were always slick and we were clumsy. Through brainwashing they were able to broadcast peace appeals by our men. What kind of appeals did we broadcast? We pleaded with twenty-two of our men who had actually transferred allegiance to the Reds, "Come home, all is forgiven." When one of them did come home, we court-martialed him—just as the Reds predicted we would! How stupid can we get? That blunder will be a windfall to the Communists' propaganda for many years.

We missed one marvelous chance to make bums out of the Reds during the long-winded truce negotiations in Korea. One of the issues on the exchange of prisoners was whether we would force thousands of unwilling former Reds to go home. There were seventy thousand prisoners who wanted to go back and one hundred thousand who didn't. We haggled for months about this.

We could have stopped the haggling and made the Reds look foolish very simply. Suppose we had secretly loaded all the seventy thousand confirmed Reds into our amphibious fleet, landed them behind the Communist lines, and just turned the whole rabble loose. Then we announce to the world, and the Chinese in particular, "These rats are so worthless that we are giving them back to you for nothing. For negotiating purposes they aren't even worth one American prisoner; you can have them free." Think of the loss of face this would involve in the Orient for every one of those seventy thousand. The Reds, carried away by their own germ-warfare lies, might have taken drastic antiseptic precau-tions!

But we can't think like that. We follow the book; our actions are unimaginative and perfectly predictable. The Reds know it and use us as if they owned us. They sold the Big Lie on the United States germ warfare to the whole Orient.

Many people ask, "Why did the Reds go to so much trouble extorting confessions which they didn't need in China or Korea and conducting classes in POW camps to 'educate' our men?" Some of our prisoners have a startling answer to this question. They say maybe the Reds were looking ten or twenty years ahead, hoping for another depression in the United States.

What you have drilled into your brain in a POW camp stays with you the rest of your life. Maybe you don't believe it for a long time. But ten or fifteen years later, if what the Reds predict about a depression comes true, then maybe seeds the Reds planted will take root and sprout. This may seem farfetched to us who live from year to year. But it isn't to Asiatics, who look at centuries as we do at months. It is typical of the difference between our propaganda and theirs.

Moralists may object to my proposal on the ground that it is always wrong to tell a lie. A lie is a deliberate false statement made with intent to deceive someone who has a right to demand the truth. What I am proposing would be done with intent to deceive nobody. It would be done to prevent colossal deceptions such as the germ-warfare lie, which all the Reds in China still believe. It would be given world-wide publicity beforehand, so the Reds would look foolish if they verified our predictions by producing this kind of confession. Past performance indicates they are far from stupid in propaganda. They are much smarter than we are.

Besides, the only truthful answers which the Reds have a right to demand from our prisoners are "name, rank, and serial number." If you insist that we must deal with devils on a moral basis, you can say, "This is a moral twist to the Big Lie technique." Call it the "sea of lies" if you want—lies that are harmless because we predict, and authorize them; daring the enemy to use them.

Others object that this proposal would open the floodgates to a lot of military information. I don't believe it. In the first place the Reds have access, through our magazines and newspapers, to more authentic military information on technical subjects than they can digest. The public-information branches of all three services compete with one another for press space, and the easiest way to sell a feature article on a military subject is to tell an editor, "This hasn't been released before; you're getting a scoop." If I were in the Red Navy, I could easily make a reputation in Moscow as the greatest spy in history. I would get assigned to Washington as naval attaché and simply do a rewrite job on stuff I can buy on any newsstand.

In regard to tactical information, no prisoner knows anything that can really affect the outcome of World War III. That will be decided by natural resources, production capacity and things that the Communists know all about from the atomic scientist, Doctor Fuchs, and others like him. To protect their own front-line units, most of our prisoners only have to keep their mouths shut for about a week. After that, tactical dispositions on the front have so changed that they can spill all they know without affecting the outcome of even a small battle one way or the other. Those who know things that might affect the future of the war, such as future tactical or strategic plans must not be allowed to subject themselves to the risk of capture.

It makes fine reading in the newspapers when General Mac-Arthur comes ashore right behind the first assault wave or General Patton barges into an enemy-held town in the lead tank. But it's a badly miscalculated risk when we permit them to do this. Sure, it's good for morale—of a limited number of front-line troops, and also of the generals concerned. But think of the shot in the arm it would be to enemy morale if they were captured. And think of the really vital military information their capture would jeopardize.

MacArthur is a brave man, and so was Patton. But they were never brainwashed. No one can say just how much they could have taken before they broke. Major tools of the brainwashing process are degradation and humiliation. Obviously, the higher a prisoner's rank, the further you can degrade him, and the easier it is to humiliate him. We say you must tell "name, rank, and serial number," but if I were ever captured, those are the three items

I would do my damndest to conceal. Maybe I could give my rank as rear admiral and claim it meant "radioman."

All our ideas about military security require a drastic overhaul. Our GIs and all our citizens know too much. We should tighten up on military information and pass it out only on a "need-to-know" basis. This would help to protect our prisoners as well as our secrets, because you can't betray a secret if you don't know it.

We might also revise our ideas on what constitutes "collaboration with the enemy" in the light of what goes on back here in these United States. Back here, during the Korean snafu, Peress stopped a Senate committee cold when they asked him if he was a Communist, by invoking the Fifth Amendment. Soon thereafter he was promoted to major and given an honorable discharge. When our captured soldiers are being brainwashed, there is no law this side of hell they can invoke. All they can do now to stop the torture is to "confess"—or die.

Our present policy of dealing with some of our own prisoners of war is a windfall to the Communists. Compare how we treat a brainwashed GI with the treatment guaranteed by the Constitution even for criminals. A soldier who had an obviously false propaganda confession tortured out of him can be tried by court-martial for giving "aid and comfort to the enemy." A criminal who has a true confession beaten out of him by the police goes scot free if he can prove that he was forced to tell the truth about an actual crime. This is one of the American rights that our soldier was defending when he got captured. I wonder how he feels when a false confession, extorted by the Reds, is produced before a United States military court composed of men who have never even seen the Reds face to face.

We didn't even brief our men consistently in Korea on what to say if captured. The Army, Navy, Air Force, and Marines all had their own ideas on this question, and different units of the same service differed. The briefings given to our men going into battle varied all the way from zero to carte blanche advice: "Spill anything you know; they know it too." The "name, rank, and serial number" briefing was stateside stuff that you got from people who knew they would never be captured. Some units avoided any briefing whatever on this question "because telling the men about Communist tortures would be bad for morale."

I agree that frank briefing on brainwashing, for men who may have to face it, probably won't make them very happy. But that's no excuse for burying our heads in the sand and trying to ignore it.

When all the brainwashers want is agreement with their ideas, their job is relatively simple. They just put the heat on you until you sign what they want. Then the interrogator has documentary proof for his commissar that he is a shrewd operator. But if they go after military information, the job is much more difficult. They have to evaluate what you say, cross-check it against known facts, and make up their own minds. Their "conditioned-reflex" technique doesn't cover this. They may have to go back to the dogs and rats in their laboratories and conduct further experiments to find out how they can tell when the animal is behaving "truthfully" rather than the way they have conditioned it to act.

Some of our expert interrogators and psychologists say there is no use trying to deceive expert interrogators: you just have to clam up and refuse to answer. If you lie, they will find you out. Our boys who went through brainwashing say that on military information, they could get away with evasive or false answers. But when the Reds demand a "yes" answer to a propaganda question, you either give it to them or else.

We can't give our boys shots so they won't be hurt when tortured, get weak when starved, or become dopey from lack of sleep. But maybe we can save them from enduring these tortures rather than confess to obvious lies. The least we can do is to assure them that whatever they say or do under these circumstances will not help the enemy, because we have disavowed it ahead of time. We can thus relieve their minds of the gnawing fear that what they say will be held against them when they get home. All our boys to whom I have talked agree that was perhaps the worst fear that haunted them during their ordeals. That is one dragon we could slay forever with an executive order.

This is one of those things on which it seems we have nothing to lose and a lot to gain. The Communists, even if they continue their brainwashing, can't treat our men any worse than they have. At the very least, we will ensure that none of our men endures the ordeal of brainwashing through fear of being stigmatized as a traitor if he signs an obvious fairy tale.

General Dean, in his book, makes this very significant statement: "One of the first things I noticed was that these people were much more anxious to have me say what they wanted me to say than to extract any really new or useful information. Pressure on me was greatest to agree to perfectly obvious falsities." Many other ex-prisoners agree that the only real heat put on them was to extract false confessions for propaganda purposes.

Our present military regulations are designed to protect military information, and all evidence shows that the Communists don't use brainwashing to get military information: they use it to get propaganda material. Why should they bother trying to extract military information from our prisoners? In a battle to conquer mankind with an idea, it doesn't pay off. If an expert interrogator pries the location of your artillery battery out of a prisoner, they may destroy or capture your battery. But under present conditions, if he pries a false confession out of him, he may capture the minds of three hundred million Asiatic people.

There is no power on this side of hell that can prevent the Reds from brainwashing and breaking a certain number of our men. But we can cut the ground out from under them for propaganda purposes, and thus destroy the usefulness of brain-wash confessions. We might spare our men a lot of heroic but utterly futile resistance to torture in the future, and ensure that never again will the Communist devils be able to make us look as bad as they made us look in Korea.

To leave the solution of this problem in military hands isn't fair to anyone concerned, including the much maligned military brass. Military men have a Spartan code of ethics of which they are justly proud, and the American people rightly expect them to live up to it. If we leave this problem in their hands, we can expect a Spartan solution, all wrapped up in a neat little ball of military wax, such as "name, rank, and serial number," for foot soldiers and the bombardier of a B-47 alike.

The problem is only partly military and it is much too big for any such pat solution as that. We have to educate the American people to realize that we aren't playing a game any more, a game that can be run by gentlemen's agreements and international pacts. We are in a life-and-death struggle with a godless system bent on world domination, a system which regards human dignity as a zero quantity.

Against the brainwashers, the Geneva Convention is as obsolete as the TNT bomb. It is our duty to the future defenders of our freedoms to find a better answer to it.

GENERAL ORDER   NAVY DEPARTMENT

NO. 4   Washington, D.C., March 18, 1957

CODE OF CONDUCT FOR MEMBERS OF THE ARMED FORCES OF THE UNITED STATES

1. The following executive order and the Code of Conduct for Members of the Armed Forces of the United States established thereby are in effect:

EXECUTIVE ORDER 10631
"CODE OF CONDUCT FOR MEMBERS OF THE ARMED FORCES OF THE UNITED STATES"

"By virtue of the authority vested in me as President of the United States, and as Commander in Chief of the Armed Forces of the United States, I hereby prescribe the Code of Conduct for Members of the Armed Forces of the United States which is attached to this order and hereby made a part thereof.

"Every member of the Armed Forces of the United States is

expected to measure up to the standards embodied in this Code of Conduct while he is in combat or in captivity. To ensure achievement of these standards, each member of the Armed Forces liable to capture shall be provided with specific training and instruction designed to better equip him to counter and withstand all enemy efforts against him, and shall be fully instructed as to the behavior and obligations expected of him during combat or captivity.

"The Secretary of Defense (and the Secretary of the Treasury with respect to the Coast Guard, except when it is serving as part of the Navy) shall take such action as is deemed necessary to implement this order and to disseminate and make the said Code known to all members of the Armed Forces of the United States."

Dwight D. Eisenhower

THE WHITE HOUSE
August 17, 1955

CODE OF CONDUCT FOR MEMBERS OF THE ARMED FORCES OF THE UNITED STATES

I

I AM AN AMERICAN FIGHTING MAN. I SERVE IN THE FORCES WHICH GUARD MY COUNTRY AND OUR WAY OF LIFE. I AM PREPARED TO GIVE MY LIFE IN THEIR DEFENSE.

A member of the Armed Forces is always a fighting man. As such, it is his duty to oppose the enemies of the United States regardless of the circumstances in which he may find himself, whether in active participation in combat, or as a prisoner of war.

II

I WILL NEVER SURRENDER OF MY OWN FREE WILL. IF IN COMMAND
I WILL NEVER SURRENDER MY MEN WHILE THEY STILL HAVE THE
MEANS TO RESIST.

As an individual, a member of the Armed Forces may never
voluntarily surrender himself. When isolated and he can no longer
inflict casualties on the enemy, it is his duty to evade capture and
rejoin the nearest friendly forces.

The responsibility and authority of a commander never extends
to the surrender of his command to the enemy while it has power
to resist or evade. When isolated, cut off, or surrounded, a unit
must continue to fight until relieved, or able to rejoin friendly
forces, by breaking out or by evading the enemy.

III

IF I AM CAPTURED I WILL CONTINUE TO RESIST BY ALL MEANS
AVAILABLE. I WILL MAKE EVERY EFFORT TO ESCAPE AND AID OTHERS
TO ESCAPE. I WILL ACCEPT NEITHER PAROLE NOR SPECIAL FAVORS
FROM THE ENEMY.

The duty of a member of the Armed Forces to continue resistance
by all means at his disposal is not lessened by the misfortune of
capture. Article 82 of the Geneva Convention pertains and must
be explained. He will escape if able to do so, and will assist
others to escape. Parole agreements are promises given the captor
by a prisoner of war upon his faith and honor, to fulfill stated
conditions, such as not to bear arms or not to escape, in consideration of special privileges, usually release from captivity or a
lessened restraint. He will never sign or enter into a parole agreement.

IV

IF I BECOME A PRISONER OF WAR, I WILL KEEP FAITH WITH MY
FELLOW PRISONERS. I WILL GIVE NO INFORMATION OR TAKE PART
IN ANY ACTION WHICH MIGHT BE HARMFUL TO MY COMRADES.
IF I AM SENIOR, I WILL TAKE COMMAND. IF NOT I WILL OBEY
THE LAWFUL ORDERS OF THOSE APPOINTED OVER ME AND WILL
BACK THEM UP IN EVERY WAY.

Informing or any other action to the detriment of a fellow
prisoner is despicable and is expressly forbidden. Prisoners of war
must avoid helping the enemy identify fellow prisoners who may
have knowledge of particular value to the enemy, and may
therefore be made to suffer coercive interrogation.

Strong leadership is essential to discipline. Without discipline,
camp organization, resistance, and even survival may be impossible.
Personal hygiene, camp sanitation, and the care of sick and
wounded are imperative. Officers and noncommissioned officers of
the United States will continue to carry out their responsibilities
and exercise their authority subsequent to capture. The senior line
officer or noncommissioned officer within the prisoner of war
camp or group of prisoners will assume command according to
rank (or precedence) without regard to Service. This responsi-
ibility and accountability may not be evaded. If the senior officer
or noncommissioned officer is incapacitated or unable to act for
any reason, command will be assumed by the next senior. If the
foregoing organization cannot be effected, an organization of elected
representatives, as provided for in Articles 79–81 Geneva Convention Relative to Treatment of Prisoners of War, or a covert
organization, or both, will be formed.

V

WHEN QUESTIONED, SHOULD I BECOME A PRISONER OF WAR, I AM
BOUND TO GIVE ONLY NAME, RANK, SERVICE NUMBER, AND DATE

OF BIRTH. I WILL EVADE ANSWERING FURTHER QUESTIONS TO THE UTMOST OF MY ABILITY. I WILL MAKE NO ORAL OR WRITTEN STATEMENTS DISLOYAL TO MY COUNTRY AND ITS ALLIES OR HARMFUL TO THEIR CAUSE.

When questioned, a prisoner of war is required by the Geneva Convention and permitted by this Code to disclose his name, rank, service number, and date of birth. A prisoner of war may also communicate with the enemy regarding his individual health or welfare as a prisoner of war and, when appropriate, on routine matters of camp administration. Oral or written confessions true or false, questionnaires, personal history statements, propaganda recordings and broadcasts, appeals to other prisoners of war, signatures to peace or surrender appeals, self-criticisms or any other oral or written communication on behalf of the enemy or critical or harmful to the United States, its allies, the Armed Forces or other prisoners are forbidden.

It is a violation of the Geneva Convention to place a prisoner of war under physical or mental torture or any other form of coercion to secure from him information of any kind. If, however, a prisoner is subjected to such treatment, he will endeavor to avoid by every means the disclosure of any information, or the making of any statement or the performance of any action harmful to the interests of the United States or its allies or which will provide aid or comfort to the enemy.

Under Communist Bloc reservations to the Geneva Convention, the signing of a confession or the making of a statement by a prisoner is likely to be used to convict him as a war criminal under the laws of his captors. This conviction has the effect of removing him from the prisoner of war status and according to this Communist Bloc device denying him any protection under terms of the Geneva Convention and repatriation until a prison sentence is served.

VI

I WILL NEVER FORGET THAT I AM AN AMERICAN FIGHTING MAN, RESPONSIBLE FOR MY ACTIONS, AND DEDICATED TO THE PRINCIPLES

WHICH MADE MY COUNTRY FREE. I WILL TRUST IN MY GOD AND
IN THE UNITED STATES OF AMERICA.

The provisions of the Uniform Code of Military Justice, whenever appropriate, continue to apply to members of the Armed
Forces while prisoners of war. Upon repatriation, the conduct of
prisoners will be examined as to the circumstances of capture
and through the period of detention with due regard for the
rights of the individual and consideration for the conditions of
captivity. A member of the Armed Forces who becomes a prisoner
of war has a continuing obligation to remain loyal to his country,
his Service, and his unit.

The life of a prisoner of war is hard. He must never give
up hope. He must resist enemy indoctrination. Prisoners of war
who stand firm and united against the enemy will aid one another
in surviving this ordeal.

Charles S. Thomas
Secretary of the Navy

C.G.O. 3   U. S. GOVERNMENT PRINTING OFFICE: 1956 0-421935

Sailing Order for *Pueblo*

PRIORITY
050512 Z

FROM: CTF NINE SIX
TO : U.S.S. *Pueblo*
INFO : AIG SEVEN SIX TWO TWO
      COMSERVGRU THREE
      DIRNSA
      DIRNAVSECGRUPAC
      COMUSKOREA
      COMNAVFORKOREA
      PACCOMELINT CENTER

ICTHYIC ONE SAILORD (C)

A. CTF 96 OPORD 301–68 NOTAL
B. PACOM ELINT CENTER 210734 Z DEC 67 PASEP NOTAL
C. CINCPACFLTINST 003120.24A
D. CINCPACFLTINST 03100.3D

   1. ICHTHYIC ONE FORMERLY PINKROOT ONE.

2. DEPART SASEBO JAPAN WHEN RFS ABOUT 8 JAN 68. CHECK OUT OF MOVREP SYSTEM AND PROCEED VIA TSUSHIMA STRAITS TO ARRIVE OPAREA MARS ABOUT 10 JAN.

3. ATTEMPT TO AVOID DETECTION BY SOVIET NAVAL UNITS WHILE PROCEEDING OPAREA MARS.

4. UPON ARRIVAL MARS, CONDUCT ICHTHYIC OPS IAW PROVISIONS REF A.

A. OPERATE OPAREAS MARS, VENUS AND PLUTO, CONCENTRATING EFFORTS AREA(S) WHICH APPEAR MOST LUCRATIVE.

B. DEPART OPAREAS 27 JAN AND IF NOT UNDER SURVEILLANCE, MAINTAIN STRICT EMCON CONDITION. PROCEED SOUTH ALONG KOREAN COAST TO VICINITY TSUSHIMA STRAITS.

C. INTERCEPT AND CONDUCT SURVEILLANCE OF SOVIET NASIMA STRAITS.

D. TERMINATE SURVEILLANCE TO ARRIVE SASEBO 4 FEB 68. EARLIER DEPARTURE AUTHORIZED TO ENSURE TEN PERCENT ON-BOARD FUEL UPON ARRIVAL SASEBO.

5. OPAREAS DEFINED AS FOLLOWS:

A. EAST/WEST BOUNDARIES ALL AREAS ARE CONTIGUOUS TO KORCOM COAST EXTENDING FROM THIRTEEN NM CPA TO LAND MASS/OFF-SHORE ISLANDS SEAWARD TO SIXTY NM.

B. NORTH/SOUTH BOUNDARIES ARE:

    MARS, 40–00N4 TO 39–00N2;

    VENUS, 41–00N5 to 40–00N4;

    PLUTO, 42–00N6 TO 41–00N5.

6. SPECIAL INSTRUCTIONS:

A. COLLECT ELINT IAW PROVISIONS REF B, ON NOT TO INTERFERE BASIS WITH BASIC MISSION.

B. CPA TO KORCOM/SOVIET LAND MASS/OFF-SHORE ISLANDS WILL BE THIRTEEN NM.

C. UPON ESTABLISHING FIRM CONTACT WITH SOVIET NAVAL UNITS, BREAK EMCON AND TRANSMIT DAILY SITREP.

D. OPERATE AT LEAST FIVE HUNDRED YDS AS NECESSARY FOR VISUAL/PHOTO COVERAGE.

E. DO NOT INTERFERE WITH SOVIET EXERCISES BUT MAINTAIN A POSITION ON THE PERIPHERY FOR OBSERVATION PURPOSES.

F. IF UNABLE TO ESTABLISH OR GAIN CONTACT WITH SOVIET UNITS WITHIN TWENTY-FOUR HOURS ARRIVAL TSUSHIMA STRAITS AREA, ADVISE ORIG. IMMEDIATE PRECEDENCE.

G. PROVISIONS REF C APPLY REGARDING RULES OF ENGAGEMENT. REF D APPLIES REGARDING CONDUCT IN EVENT OF HARASSMENT OR INTIMIDATION BY FOREIGN UNITS.

H. INSTALLED DEFENSE ARMAMENT SHOULD BE STOWED OR COVERED IN SUCH A MANNER AS TO NOT ELICIT UNUSUAL INTEREST FROM SURVEYING/SURVEYED UNIT(S). EMPLOY ONLY IN CASES WHERE THREAT TO SURVIVAL IS OBVIOUS.

Pueblo's Radio Transmissions

DEPARTMENT OF THE NAVY
OFFICE OF THE CHIEF OF NAVAL OPERATIONS
WASHINGTON, D.C. 20350

IN REPLY REFER TO
Op–03Pl: gm
Memo 457–69
13 March 1969

UNCLASSIFIED

MEMORANDUM FOR MR. FRANK SLATINSHEK (STAFF COUNSEL, SPECIAL SUBCOMMITTEE, Pueblo INQUIRY)

Subj: *Pueblo* Incident (U)
Encl: (L) Chronology of Radio Transmissions to and from the *Pueblo* pertinent to the seizure

1. Enclosure (1) is forwarded herewith as requested.

(s)
LESLIE J. O'BRIEN, JR.,
Rear Admiral, U. S. Navy
Special Assistant to the Chief of Naval Operations
for *Pueblo* Matters

UNCLASSIFIED

Chronology of all radio transmissions to and from the *Pueblo* pertinent to the seizure commencing the day before the seizure through the time *Pueblo* went off the air.

1. *Background.*

a. The first record of contact by *Pueblo* with a shore station is approximately 0920Z/22 JAN (1820 local). At this time *Pueblo* broke radio silence and called NAVCOMMSTA JAPAN on primary CW ship to shore (1306 KHz) and requested activation of 100 wpm ORESTES covered communications with Kamiseya. This was in accordance with her communications instructions.

b. Communications from ship to the shore in this area is sometimes difficult due to the propagation conditions which vary with the different times of the day. According to the reports from the commanding officer of the Naval Communication Station in Japan, communications to some of the areas from the Sea of Japan are not always satisfactory. That is, selection of the proper frequencies vary for use at different times throughout the day. It is necessary that ships have available to them a selection from a wide range of frequencies in order to maintain communications reliably under those poor propagation conditions. Thirteen different frequencies were tried prior to establishment of a two-way circuit with *Pueblo.*

c. The circuit was established at 1054 Korean local time on 23 January 1968. This circuit was a 100 word-per-minute, simplex (one-way reversible), crypto-covered, high frequency radio teletype circuit. The circuit was activated continuously from 1054 until 1432 when *Pueblo* went off the air to destroy the crypto equipment.

d. The following chronology picks up with *Pueblo's* transmission of SITREP 1 at 231100 Korean time. Korean local time is used throughout except date-time groups are given in GMT(Z) and Korean local time.

2. *Chronology*

Korean
Local
Time   *Transmissions*   *Actions Taken*

1100   *Pueblo* completed transmission   CNF (CTF–96) Watch
       of SITREP 1 (DTG 220915 Z).   Officer Intelligence read/
       This report was addressed to   filed on interest board.
       AIG 7622.

1135   *Pueblo* completed transmission   Routine patrol; no action
       of Intel/Tech Rpt ⌗1 (DTG   required.
       220820 Z/221720 Korean). Pre-
       cedence was Routine and mes-
       sage was addressed to fifteen
       activities.

1140   *Pueblo* completed service mes-   Routine action taken to re-
       sage (a request for missing   broadcast missing numbers
       COPI   broadcast   numbers)   requested.
       (DTG 221126 Z/222026 Ko-
       rean).

1150   *Pueblo* completed transmission   CNFJ (CTF–96) Watch
       of SITREP 2 (DTG 230150 Z/   officers in Intelligence read
       231050 Korean). This report   /filed on interest board.
       had Priority precedence and
       was addressed for action to
       CTF–96 and to the following
       for information:

COMMANDING GENERAL, FIFTH AIR FORCE
COMMANDER IN CHIEF, PACIFIC
COMMANDER IN CHIEF, PACIFIC AIR FORCE

COMMANDER IN CHIEF, U. S. PACIFIC FLEET
CHIEF OF NAVAL OPERATIONS
COMMANDER, FLEET AIR WING SIX
COMMANDER SERVICE FORCE, U. S. PACIFIC FLEET
COMMANDER, SEVENTH FLEET
DIRECTOR, NAVAL SECURITY GROUP
FLEET AIR RECONNAISSANCE SQUADRON ONE
HEADQUARTERS, NATIONAL SECURITY AGENCY, PACIFIC
JOINT CHIEFS OF STAFF
NAVAL FIELD OPERATIONS INTELLIGENCE OFFICE
NAVAL SECURITY GROUP ACTIVITY (KAMISEYA)
OCEANOGRAPHER OF THE NAVY

1200   *Pueblo* operator stated he had another message being prepared for transmission and that there was "COMPANY OUTSIDE."

1210   *Pueblo* transmitted INTEL/TECH REPT number 2 (DTG 230206 Z/231106 Korean). For period 220001 Z–222400 Z. Precedence was Routine and message was addressed to several (15) intelligence activities.

        Routine patrol; no action required as indicated.

1210–   Exchange of transmissions be-
1244   tween *Pueblo* and Kamiseya operators regarding garbled or misunderstood portions of four messages sent by *Pueblo;* reruns of parts of messages, checks of routing indicators assigned, etc. At approximately 1230, *Pueblo* operator advised, "DON'T WANT TO GO DOWN YET. WE STILL GOT

COMPANY OUTSIDE. WILL ADVISE ASAP."

1244   *Pueblo* operator advised, "WE ARE FINISHED FOR NOW BUT GOT COMPANY OUTSIDE AND MORE COMING SO WILL HAVE TO KEEP THIS UP FOR A WHILE. WILL ADVISE ASAP."

1245–   Exchange of transmissions be-
1249   tween operators, primarily personnel chatter, such as; sea duty is rough, be glad to get back, see you about 7 FEB, etc. At end of period, *Pueblo* operator sent, "I AM TRYING TO FIND OUT WHAT THE OIC WANTS (Garble) NOW BUT EVERYONE IS TOPSIDE WORRYING (Garble) HAVE RIGHT NOW WILL ADVISE ASAP." This was followed shortly by, "CHANGE YOUR TAPE AND GOT A FLASH COMING FOR YOU NOW. AM GETTING IT READY NOW. STANDBY FOR FLASH."

1250–   *Pueblo* transmitted OPREP 3/
1254   PINNACLE 1 message (DTG 230352 Z/231252 Korean) twice and Kamiseya receipted at 1254. Kamiseya advised, "FLASH GONE," indicating message was being relayed.

1255–   *Pueblo* operator advised, "GOT   PINNACLE 1 was re-
1315   SOME MORE COMING SOON SO   ceived by CNFJ at 1313

WILL HAVE TO STAY UP. WILL ADVISE WHEN WE GET READY FOR YOU." Kamiseya acknowledged this and requested a rerun of a line from a previous message. *Pueblo* complied. Kamiseya acknowledged and sent, "DO YOU HAVE ANYMORE TRAFFIC? HOW IT FEEL TO BE THREATENED?" *Pueblo* response was, "GOT SOME MORE COMING IN A MINUTE BUT DON'T HAVE IT IN COMM YET. WILL PASS IT AS SOON AS I GET. IT IS WORSE OUT HERE NOW, GOT MORE COMPANY AND NOT DOING SO GOOD WITH THEM SO WILL HAVE TO KEEP THIS CIRCUIT UP, WILL ADVISE ASAP AND PLEASE STAY WITH ME ON CIRCUIT."

and hand-delivered to Chief of Staff by Intelligence watch officer. Also delivered to OPCONCENTER Harassment reported was no worse than expected nor as bad as previously experienced by *Banner* (AGER 1).

1315– Kamiseya acknowledged the
1317 above and sent, "KNOW WHAT YOU MEAN ABOUT THAT COMPANY AND WILL STAY DOWN SO YOU CAN COME TO ME. HOW TO PUT ON TEST ON YOUR NEXT START UNTIL YOU GET YOUR TRAFFIC SO WE CAN KEEP FREQ FAIRLY CLEAR?" *Pueblo* complied and ran a test tape for about a minute.

1318– *Pueblo* transmitted OPREP
1321 3/PINNACLE 2 message

Kamiseya relayed message to CNFJ, who received at

(DTG 230415 Z/231315 Korean) once and Kamiseya receipted. *Pueblo* voluntarily retransmitted the message. This message was the first indication that more than harassment was involved.

1322– No transmission between *Pueblo*
1325 and Kamiseya other than repeats of PINNACLE 2.

1326– *Pueblo* sent, "AND THEY PLAN
1327 TO OPEN FIRE ON US NOW, THEY PLAN TO OPEN FIRE ON US NOW, THEY PLAN TO OPEN FIRE ON US NOW."

1328 *Pueblo* again commenced sending PINNACLE 2 but interrupted to send, "NORTH KOREAN WAR VESSELS PLAN TO OPEN FIRE, SHIP POSIT 39–25.5N, 127–54.9E, SHIP POSIT 39–25.5N, 127–54.9E." Kamiseya acknowledged this and asked, "HOW MANY FLASH HAVE YOU SENT US?" Kamiseya continued to acknowledge receipt of *Pueblo* posit info, and invited *Pueblo* to transmit.

1330 *Pueblo* transmitted, "WE ARE BEING BOARDED," five times followed by two repeats of pre-

1322. Intelligence watch officer hand-delivered to Chief of Staff who ordered, "RELAY INFO TO 5th AF AND PUSH THE BUTTON FOR CONTINGENCY ACTION."

Kamiseya received at 1328 and relayed it CNFJ who received at 1329. Based on this and PINNACLE 2, CNFJ prepared to send a special procedure message

Kamiseya was now relaying all *Pueblo* transmissions in near real time to CNFJ by secure teletype circuit. At 1330 CNFJ initiated first phone call (secure) to 5 AF HQ for assistance.

vious ship's position, and two repeats of, "WE ARE BEING BOARDED." "SOS" was then sent thirteen times, followed by two transmissions of a revised ship's position, "39–34N, 127–54E," eighteen more SOSs and the new position once more. Kamiseya acknowledged receipt of all these transmissions and invited *Pueblo* to continue sending.

1331   *Pueblo* resumed transmitting a few minutes later with, "WE ARE HOLDING EMERGENCY DESTRUCTION. WE NEED HELP. WE ARE HOLDING EMERGENCY DESTRUCTION. WE NEED SUPPORT. SOS SOS SOS. PLEASE SEND ASSISTANCE (sent four times), SOS, SOS, SOS. WE ARE BEING BOARDED. HOLDING EMERGENCY DESTRUCTION." Kamiseya acknowledged and again invited *Pueblo* to continue sending.

At 1335, CNFJ transmitted a special procedure message based on contents of PINNACLE 2 and "chatter" from *Pueblo*.

1331–   At about 1337, *Pueblo* advised,
1337   "WE ARE LAYING TO AT PRESENT POSITION. AS OF YET WE NO LONGER HAVE GOPI (WESTPAC-OPINTEL broadcast). THIS CIRCUIT ONLY CIRCUIT ACTIVE ON NIP. PLEASE SEND ASSISTANCE. WE ARE BEING BOARDED."

1338   Kamiseya responded to last *Pueblo* transmission "QSL (roger) YOUR LAST AND PASSING ALL INFO." No other transmissions this period, except a call by Kamiseya for *Pueblo* to transmit.

Kamiseya readdressed PINNACLE 2 as a special procedure message at 1338. At 1340 Kamiseya readdressed PINNACLE 1 as a special procedure message.

1345–   At 1345 *Pueblo* advised, "WE
1409   ARE BEING ESCORTED INTO PROB WONSON REPEAT WONSON. WE ARE BEING ESCORTED INTO PROB WONSON REPEAT WONSON." Kamiseya acknowledged this transmission and the following exchange took place for the remainder of the period:

1. At 1346 CNFJ initiated a second special procedure message based on *Pueblo* chatter about boarding.

Pueblo—"ARE YOU SENDING ASSISTANCE" (four times).

2. Subsequently, a total of 15 "follow-ups" special procedure were originated by CNFJ and Kamiseya, based on "chatter" from *Pueblo*.

Kamiseya—"WORD HAS GONE TO ALL AUTHORITIES. WORD HAS GONE TO ALL AUTHORITIES. COMNAVFORJAPAN IS REQUESTING ASSIT. WHAT KEY LIST DO YOU HAVE LEFT?"

"LAST WE GOT FROM YOU WAS 'ARE YOU SENDING ASSIT.' PLEASE ADVISE WHAT KEY LIST YOU HAVE LEFT AND IF IT APPEARS THAT YOUR COMM SPACES WILL BE ENTERED?"

3. Throughout the period CNFJ made several telephone calls to Commander, 5th AF with respect to AF assistance. At 1350 5th AF HQ advised no aircraft on alert.

Pueblo—"HAVE O KEYLIST AND THIS ONLY ONE HAVE, HAVE BEEN REQUESTED TO FOLLOW INTO WONSON, HAVE THREE WOUNDED AND ONE MAN WITH LEG BLOWN OFF, HAVE NOT USED ANY WEAPONS OR UNCOVERED 50-CAL. MAC. DESTROYING ALL KEYLISTS AND AS MUCH ELE EQUIPT AS POSSIBLE. HOW ABOUT SOME HELP, THESE GUYS MEAN BUSINESS. HAVE SUSTAINED SMALL WOUND IN RECTUM, DO NOT INTEND TO OFFER ANY RESISTANCE. INTERROGATIVE QSL.° INTERROGATIVE QSL. DO NOT KNOW HOW LONG WILL BE ABLE TO HOLD UP CIRCUIT AND DO NOT KNOW IF COMM SPACES WILL BE ENTERED."

Kamiseya—"ROGER, ROGER. WE DOING ALL WE CAN. CAPT HERE AND CNFJ ON HOTLINE. LAST I GOT WAS AIR FORCE GOING HELP YOU WITH SOME AIRCRAFT BUT CAN'T REALLY SAY AS CNFJ COORDINATING WITH I PRESUME KOREA FOR SOME F-105. THIS UNOFFICIAL BUT I THINK THAT WHAT WILL HAPPEN."

Pueblo—"ROGER YOUR LAST. ROGER YOUR LAST."

1410 Kamiseya sent, "STILL READ YOU QRK FIVER FIVER. GO AHEAD

KEEP KW-7 ON THE AIR LONG
AS YOU CAN. WE STAYING RIGHT
WITH YOU."

1411 *Pueblo* sent, "ROGER, ROGER,
WILL KEEP THIS UP UNTIL LAST
MINUTE WILL STAY UP UNTIL
THE LAST MINUTE AND SURE
COULD USE SOME HELP NOW."

1412 Kamiseya sent, "ROGER, ROGER.
WE STILL WITH YOU AND DOING
ALL WE CAN. EVERYONE REALLY
TURNING TO AND FIGURE BY
NOW AIR FORCE GOT SOME BIRDS
WINGING YOUR WAY."

At 1412, Kamiseya commenced passing chatter to Com7THFLT via torn-tape relay at HAVCOMM-STA PHIL.

1413 *Pueblo* sent, "ROGER, ROGER,
SURE HOPE SO. WE PRETTY BUSY
WITH DESTRUCTION RIGHT NOW.
CAN'T SEE FOR THE SMOKE."

1414 Kamiseya sent, "ROGER, ROGER,
WISH I COULD HELP MORE. ALL
INFO YOU PASS BEING SENT TO
AREA COMMANDER AND THEY
IN TURN CO-ORDINATING FOR
WHATEVER ACTION GOT TO BE
TAKEN. SURE PROCESS ALREADY
BEING INITIATED FOR SOME IM-
MEDIATE RELIEF. COMSEVENTH-
FLT, CNFJ, AND NSA GROUP PAC
ALL GOT INFO RIGHT AWAY."

1415 *Pueblo* sent, "ROGER YOUR LAST
AND SURE HOPE SOMEONE DOES
SOMETHING. WE ARE HELPLESS
AT THIS TIME. CANNOT DO ANY-
THING BUT WAIT."

1417 Kamiseya sent, "WHO I GOT THAT END OF CIRCUIT. WHAT STATUS OF CLASSIFIED MATERIAL LEFT TO DESTROY?"

1418 *Pueblo* sent, "WE HAVE THE KW-7 AND SOME CARDS IN THE 37 AND 14 (crypto equipments KWR-37 and KG-14) TO SMASH. I THINK THAT JUST ABOUT IT."

1419 Kamiseya sent, "RIGHT. CONTINUE TO HANG TO P & I BUTTON. WE BE RIGHT THERE. YOUR SIGNAL MIGHTY GOOD AND HOPE STAYS THAT WAY. YOU GOT ANY FURTHER INFO THAT MIGHT HELP EVALUATE SITUATION?" *Pueblo* sent, "ROGER YOUR LAST. WILL STAY WITH AS LONG AS I CAN. WILL PUT (garble) ON AND LEAVE THEM UNTIL I NEED YOU."

1420 Kamiseya sent, "CNFJ ADVISED FIFTH AIR FORCE ALERTED REPEAT CNFJ ADVISED FIFTH AIR FORCE ALERTED."

At 1420 CNFJ notifies CINCPACFLT of incident by secure phone.

1421– *Pueblo* made transmission that
1427 was completely garbled and unreadable. Kamiseya made several requests for a repeat.

1428 Kamiseya sent twice, "IF OPERATIONS PERMIT, CAN YOU PROVIDE CURRENT SITREP INCLUD-

ING INTENTIONS KORCOMS IF POSSIBLE, DAMAGE, AND INJURIES SUSTAINED."

1430 *Pueblo* sent, "ROGER AND DESTRUCTION OF PUBS HAVE BEEN INEFFECTIVE. SUSPECT SEVERAL WILL BE COMPROMISED." Kamiseya sent twice, "CAN YOU GIVE ME A LIST OF WHAT YOU HAVEN'T DESTROYED?"

1432 *Pueblo* sent, "HAVE BEEN DIRECTED TO COME TO ALL STOP AND BEING BOARDED AT THIS TIME. BEING BOARDED AT THIS TIME." Kamiseya sent, "ROGER YOUR LAST. IT ON WAY TO CNFJ." *Pueblo* sent, "FOUR MEN INJURED AND ONE CRITICALLY AND GOING OFF THE AIR NOW AND DESTROYING THIS GEAR." (last transmission) Kamiseya sent, "ROGER, GO AHEAD. CAN YOU TRANSMIT IN THE CLEAR?" Kamiseya repeated calls for the *Pueblo* to transmit in the clear for several hours.

3. *Analysis*—What actions were possible?
   Time to act before dark. 231330 to 231806=4^h 36^m
   Time to act before seizure. 231330 to 231435=1^h 5^m
   Time to act until *Pueblo* abeam Ung Do island.
      231330 to 231645=3^h 15^m
   Time to act until *Pueblo* moored at the pier.
      231330 to 232030=7^h

May 6, 1969

Statement of John H. Chafee,
Secretary of the Navy,
on *Pueblo* Court of Inquiry

The court of inquiry convened by the United States Navy to inquire into the seizure of U.S.S. *Pueblo* by North Korean forces on January 23, 1968, has completed its proceedings. It has carried out this complex and difficult assignment with commendable thoroughness, objectivity, and professional skill. Its report has been submitted to higher naval authorities for review.

The record of the court of inquiry will be of continuing value in the Navy's re-examination of concepts, policies, regulations, and procedures which had a bearing on the *Pueblo* incident. A variety of corrective actions have flowed and will flow from it.

Higher naval authorities have completed their review of the disciplinary aspects of the record, as I personally have also done. My review was of course limited to the evidence and to the findings, opinions, and recommendations of this court of inquiry and the recommendations of the subsequent reviewing authorities.

As a result of my review, I have decided that no disciplinary action will be taken against any of the personnel involved in the *Pueblo* incident. I will first give you the conclusions of the court

of inquiry, the Convening Authority, and the Chief of Naval
Operations, then explain the basis for my decision.

Based upon its findings of fact and the formal opinions which it
derived from those findings, the court of inquiry recommended that
Commander Lloyd M. Bucher, U. S. Navy, the commanding
officer of U.S.S. *Pueblo*, be brought to trial by general court-
martial for the following *five alleged offenses: permitting his
ship to be searched while he had the power to resist; failing to
take immediate and aggressive protective measures when his ship
was attacked by North Korean forces; complying with the orders
of the North Korean forces to follow them into port; negligently
failing to complete destruction of classified material aboard U.S.S.*
Pueblo *and permitting such material to fall into the hands of the
North Koreans; and negligently failing to ensure, before departure
for sea, that his officers and crew were properly organized, sta-
tioned, and trained in preparation for emergency destruction of
classified material.*

*The court of inquiry also recommended that Lieutenant Stephen
R. Harris, U. S. Naval Reserve, the officer-in-charge of the research
detachment aboard U.S.S.* Pueblo, *be brought to trial by general
court-martial for three alleged offenses of dereliction in the per-
formances of his duties, in that he failed to inform the commanding
officer of* Pueblo *of a certain deficiency in the classified support
capabilities of the research detachment; failed to train and drill
the research detachment properly in emergency destruction procedures; and failed to take effective action to complete emergency
destruction after having been ordered by the commanding officer
to dispose of all remaining classified materials.*

It was recommended by the court of inquiry that Lieutenant
Edward R. Murphy, Jr., U. S. Navy, the executive officer of
U.S.S. *Pueblo*, be given nonjudicial punishment in the form of
a letter of admonition for *alleged dereliction in the performance
of his duties as executive officer, in that he negligently failed to
organize and lead the crew on the day of seizure, especially*

in the ship's major internal task of emergency destruction of classi-
fied material.

The court of inquiry recommended that Rear Admiral Frank L.
Johnson, U. S. Navy, and Captain Everett B. Gladding, U. S.
Navy (retired), each receive nonjudicial punishment in *the form
of a letter of reprimand. The court alleged that Rear Admiral
Johnson, then Commander Naval Forces, Japan, was derelict in
the performance of duty in negligently failing to plan properly
for effective emergency support forces for contingencies such as
occurred during the execution of* Pueblo's *mission, and negligently
failing to verify effectively the feasibility of rapid emergency
destruction of classified equipment and documents carried by the*
Pueblo *research detachment. In the case of Captain Gladding,
then Director Naval Security Group, Pacific, it was alleged that
he was derelict in the performance of duty in negligently failing
to develop procedures to ensure the readiness of* Pueblo's *research
detachment for the mission assigned, and to co-ordinate other
services and agencies to provide intelligence support to* Pueblo
during the mission.

The completely objective approach of the court of inquiry to
its duties was clearly reflected in its full presentation of factors
which would have mitigating effect with respect to the offenses
alleged. Note was taken of such matters as the recent change in
policy which resulted in the last-minute installation of armament
aboard *Pueblo;* the limitations and deficiencies of that armament
installation and of *Pueblo's* other defensive capabilities; the emphasis placed by superior commanders upon the importance of
restraint and nonprovocation under harassment; the limitations and
deficiencies of *Pueblo's* facilities for emergency destruction of classified materials, and of the Navy's planning therefor; the absence
of centralized control of the amount of classified materials required
to be carried by intelligence-collection ships; the failure of other
responsible authorities to provide proper support; and the 160
years of precedent which was shattered when *Pueblo* was seized
by an act of piracy on the high seas in clear violation of international law.

The Commander in Chief of the U. S. Pacific Fleet, as Convening Authority, declined to accept the recommendations of the court of inquiry that Commander Bucher and Lieutenant Harris be brought to trial by general court-martial. He recommended instead a proceeding of lesser measure—namely, the institution of formal procedures with a view to the nonjudicial punishment of each of those officers through issuance of a letter of reprimand for his alleged derelictions of duty. The Convening Authority concurred in the recommendation of the court of inquiry that Lieutenant Murphy be processed with a view to nonjudicial punishment in the form of a letter of admonition. He likewise concurred in the recommendation of the court of inquiry that procedures be instituted with a view to the issuance of a letter of reprimand to Rear Admiral Johnson—but only for the alleged dereliction of failing to verify *Pueblo*'s capability for rapid emergency destruction of classified materials. The Convening Authority recommended against the institution of procedures with a view to the issuance of a letter of reprimand to Captain Gladding.

The Chief of Naval Operations concurred in the recommendations of the Commander in Chief of the Pacific Fleet.

I have reviewed the record of the court of inquiry and the recommendations of the Convening Authority and the Chief of Naval Operations. I make no judgment regarding the guilt or innocence of any of the officers of the offenses alleged against them. Such judgment could legitimately be reached by duly constituted authority only after further legal proceedings, such as trial by court-martial or the hearing required prior to issuance of a letter of reprimand or admonition.

I am convinced, however, that neither individual discipline, nor the state of discipline or morale in the Navy, nor any other interest requires further legal proceedings with respect to any personnel involved in the Pueblo *incident.*

In reviewing the court's recommendations with respect to Commander Bucher, Lieutenant Murphy, and Lieutenant Harris, it is my opinion that—even assuming that further proceedings were had, and even going so far as to assume that a judgment of guilt were to be reached—*they have suffered enough, and further punishment would not be justified.* These officers were illegally imprisoned by the North Koreans for eleven months. During that time, their food and living conditions were marginal. They suffered extensively from physical abuse and torturous treatment. Their captors refused to accord them even the minimal humane treatment required under international law. When they were released from their captive status, each showed great loss of weight and other marks of cruel treatment.

The court was of the opinion that, during his internment, Commander Bucher upheld morale in a superior manner; that he provided leadership by insisting that command structure be maintained and providing guidance for conduct; and that he contributed to the ability of the crew to hold together and withstand the trials of detention until repatriation could be effected.

The charges against Rear Admiral Johnson and Captain Gladding relate to the failure to anticipate the emergency that subsequently developed. *This basic, general accusation, however, could be leveled in various degrees at responsible superior authorities in the chain of command and control and in the collateral support structure.*

The major factor which led to the *Pueblo*'s lonely confrontation by unanticipatedly bold and hostile forces was the sudden collapse of a premise which had been assumed at every level of responsibility and upon which every other aspect of the mission had been based—freedom of the high seas. At that particular point in history, the common confidence in the historic inviolability of a sovereign ship on the high seas in peacetime was shown to have been misplaced. The consequences must in fairness be borne by all, rather than by one or two individuals whom circumstances had placed closer to the crucial event.

In light of the considerations set out above, *I have determined that the charges against all of the officers concerned will be dismissed, and I have directed the Chief of Naval Operations to take appropriate action to that end.*

Every feasible effort is being made to correct any Navy deficiencies which may have contributed to *Pueblo*'s seizure. The Navy's leaders are determined that the lessons learned from this tragedy shall be translated into effective action.

SIG: JOHN H. CHAFEE